AN ORGANIZATIONAL APPROACH TO WORKPLACE
BULLYING

A Guide to Prevention and Management of Workplace Bullying

Dr. Debra Stewart
PSY.D., MBA, MATLT. BS

ISBN 978-1-959182-99-3 (paperback)
ISBN 978-1-960546-00-5 (hardcover)
ISBN 978-1-960546-01-2 (digital)

Rushmore Press LLC
1 800 460 9188
www.rushmorepress.com

Printed in the United States of America

An Organizational Approach to Workplace Bullying is dedicated to my son, daughter-in-law, daughter and son-in-law, and my grandchildren, who have been the greatest joys in my life. A special thank you also to my partner Gary Deaton, who encouraged me to share the work with others.

CONTENTS

THE AUTHOR'S PURPOSE IN WRITING

An Organizational Approach to Workplace Bullying

The author's experience with bullying began with being lost in the foster system as a half-blood American Indian until she was almost eight years old—not enough Indian blood to return to her people and not enough white blood to be considered adoptable. She was sent to a woman's work farm at the age of two, where the unspeakable occurred by bullies who operated without restraint and compassion for life. The author has finally gathered the right tools to stop organizational bullying from happening to others. An Organizational Approach to Workplace Bullying was written to break the cycle of abuse for organizations and corporations. The book is an edited and complete manual and has vivid application for foster homes, schools, abusive relationships, and the protection of the marginalized.

ACKNOWLEDGMENT

The strategic tools used in *An Organizational Approach to Workplace Bullying* are based on the author's information while achieving a master's in business administration and working on a doctorate in organizational psychology from Ashford University and the University of the Rockies. These educational programs detail methods to heal and promote healthy workplace cultures. I am deeply grateful for all my teachers at Ashford Forbes School of Business and the University of the Rockies. I am also thankful to numerous friends and colleagues who encouraged and supported me in writing *An Organizational Approach to Workplace Bullying.*

I owe a debt of gratitude to Dr. Dennis O'Grady, who has greatly influenced my ability to improve my interpersonal and intrapersonal communication with his TALK2Me system. Dr. O'Grady helped me realize that communication is an attitude that can heal relationships and provide the basis for effective professional communication when communicator styles are understood and respected. Ideally, as we grow with the TALK2Me communicator system, we adopt the functional aspects of both communicator styles.

Bill Witte and his Vital Life Community concept have transformed my leadership focus from innovation and productivity to include a thought process that develops a concern for how these elements are achieved and to what expense. The Vital Life Community concept focuses on socialization and well-being to create a life plan congruent with organizational and personal goals and dreams, rather than seeking socialization and well-being only if we have time.

Change occurs in a Vital Life Community or organization, so those bully triads, which consist of the bully, the victim, and the bystander, are dismantled peacefully. Thus, bully-free sectors are allowed to become leaders who respect human doing and the human being.

I want to offer my appreciation to my brother, Pastor Dan Hicks, for sharing with me the passages in the Bible that defined the bully and the importance of labeling the actions that lead to a lack of reverence in the workplace. The feelings left behind after a bully event are difficult to dismiss; however, with proper direction and focus, bully triads can move forward if they learn forgiveness. Pastor Dan Hicks has dedicated his life to the support and protection of the marginalized and to helping individuals with the process of forgiveness.

THE BULLY PROFILE

It is difficult to profile a workplace bully because of many workplace environment variables, individual unmet needs, and the lack of home and community support. Through research, the elements, traits, and personalities listed in the bully profile may easily explain the abnormal behaviors and actions of the workplace bully; however, these profile elements may also exist in any employee and those who do not create issues in the workplace. The book *An Organizational Approach to Bully* will look at the systems in the workplace that allow or encourage predatory and other bully-type behaviors.

Before we begin, unless leaders have the credentials and license to diagnose and treat personality disorders and maladaptive behaviors, it is best to explore what processes in the workplace aggravate each element of the bully profile. For example, how did the bully gain or create power inequalities in the workplace? A question for leaders to explore is what policy or procedure or reward and recognition program created the imbalance. Perhaps, the problem is a diversity and inclusion problem, and the bully just took advantage of an existing condition. Rather than fire the bully, it might be better to look at the workplace culture and find ways for the environment to be inclusive and safe for all employees. Rigorously surveying the employee population and enhancing leadership diversity and inclusion training would be a great start when addressing power inequalities in the workplace.

In the chapters that follow, the book will explore the impact of having bullies in the workplace to review the other members of the bully event, the victim and the bystander. Assessment tools provided to use or adapt, with the emphasis on training and changing the workplace culture to become bully-free. Other factors of bully prevention are the introduction of gratitude and forgiveness in the workplace so that relationships may heal.

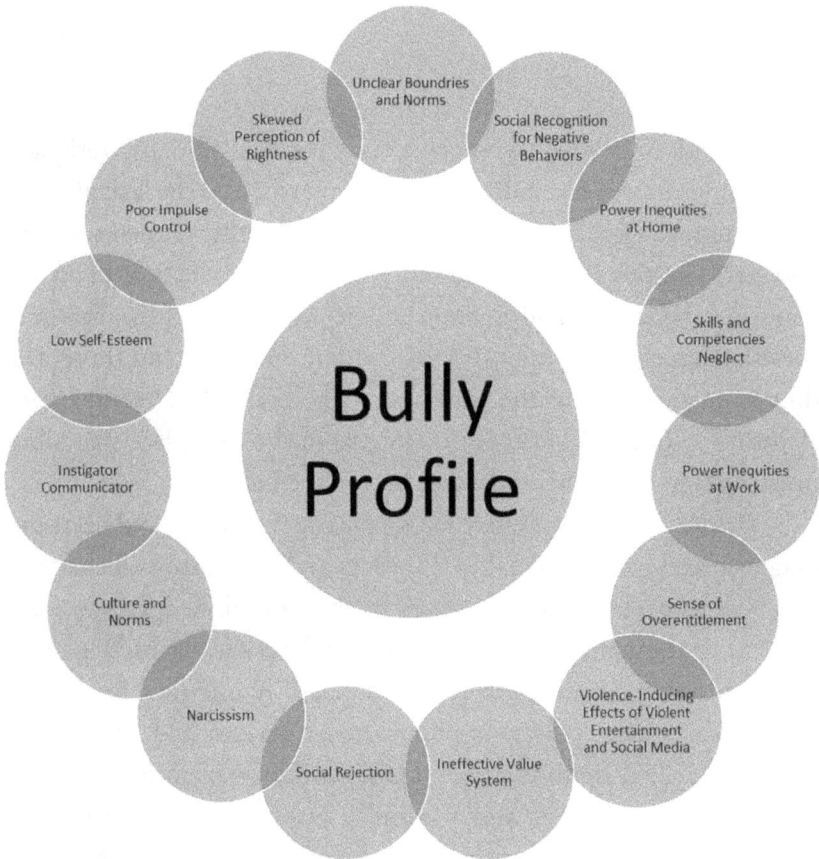

Bully Profile

- Unclear Boundries and Norms
- Skewed Perception of Rightness
- Social Recognition for Negative Behaviors
- Poor Impulse Control
- Power Inequities at Home
- Low Self-Esteem
- Skills and Competencies Neglect
- Instigator Communicator
- Power Inequities at Work
- Culture and Norms
- Sense of Overentitlement
- Narcissism
- Violence-Inducing Effects of Violent Entertainment and Social Media
- Social Rejection
- Ineffective Value System

CHAPTER 1

The Bully Impact

Organizational leaders examine and analyze the workplace environment for anything that may hinder brand image, retention of brand knowledge, productivity, and retention of human resource talent, employee satisfaction, and customer satisfaction. Additionally, factors that may obscure the mission and values of the organization are scoured for rightness and possible ethical dilemma. When factors that create any different vision are found, issues are often addressed terminally and quickly without investigating the origin. When elements are found in disharmony with the desired present and future organizational stories and memories, the culture is considered toxic and unhealthy.

Organizational administrators often stand ready to adapt to costly new management and leadership programs to offset the rising cost of doing business in a toxic environment, enlisting consultants to diagnose organizational culture and to produce treatment plans filled with cognitive-behavioral approaches that are vague and short-lived. While some consulting expense is necessary, organizational leaders may be missing the easiest of all remedies for toxic work environments and the escalating cost of doing business within an industry, which can be found in the book titled *An Organizational Approach to Workplace Bullying.*

Finding the good in the workplace bully sounds like a misnomer; however, bullies are only using skills and talents inappropriately. It is known that bully manipulation and misuse of power can devastate work teams and organizational culture. What if those same energies and skills were used appropriately and without the unrestrained ego, greed, and self-centeredness found within carefully planned and executed bully events? What if, instead of having a talent for setting up dirty alliances and bully intentions, the brutal wit of the bully was reorganized and aligned with the mission and values of the organization? *An Organizational Approach to Workplace Bullying* looks at the potential found in the bully and the need to fix the culture before considering termination of the bully.

The workplace bully can easily be identified when there are escalations in chaos and workplace tension. Bullies are often central figures who receive credit for all infamous deeds and, sometimes, heroics. However, bullies harbor resources, information, and knowledge and undermine every operational process. However, workplace bullies do not suddenly emerge into existence but are fueled by imbalances in the organizational culture and slowly nurtured to take their unfair share of the workplace power. What is the definition of a workplace bully? It depends on the organizational structure, mission, and values and how acts of aggression and misuse of power are named. Some organizations would not recognize a bully rising to power because bullies exude magnificence while riding on coworkers' skills, competencies, and talents to save the day. Other organizations would quickly sense that something was wrong because of the shift from the mission and vision and decreased employee satisfaction and loyalty.

Unless bullies get through the screening process, bullies are often created by the organization. Obviously, bullies are not hired on purpose. Bully-type personalities may be the result of possessing gifts that have not been truly developed or supported by managerial training involving emotional intelligence and critical thinking. Unbridled drive and enthusiasm for power and success may be easily interpreted as aggressive behavior if not polished by education, knowledge, and leadership training. Alternatively, bully-type personalities may arise from lack of job security and unfounded fears of demotion or being underappreciated, as evidenced by a lack of acknowledgment and reward, which may leave the bully in a desperate state of trying to find acceptance and self-actualization.

Obviously, bullies cannot work alone. A triad exists when bullies are present in the work environment, and the triad consists of the bully, the victim, and the bystander. All three groups represent an insidious discontent that overshadows positive efforts to develop a healthy workplace culture. Additionally, when bullies are left to their own devices, victims and bystanders begin mimicking the abuser, further degrading the workplace environment. Finally, toxic environments create health and wellness issues that increase healthcare costs and wreak havoc on talent retention and brand knowledge.[1] Absenteeism and accident and injury are also likely to be dominant when a bully is in the workplace. For example, depression, role clarity, stress, burnout, and fatigue are just a few of the symptoms that finally become part of the demise of the organizational culture when the bully is left unchecked.[2]

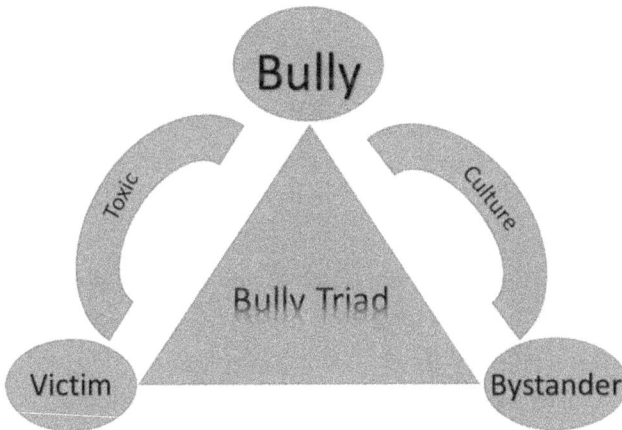

Bullies can be found in every organization and level of operation, and bullying can result in behaviors that range from being openly hostile to discreetly manipulative. For example, women are bullied more often than men, and women-to-women bullying is more common than men bullying other men.[3] Bullies are more likely found in management, and they tend to create an infrastructure of bully-like controls. The fortress that bullies create may be maintained as they continue to pillage other peaceful areas in the workplace. The infrastructure may consist of faulty performance review processes, unrealistic employee goal setting and promoting a culture of faultfinding and distrust. Also, administrators often see the bully as an internal misfit, but bullies may also work outside the organizational structure to reduce external customer satisfaction and investor confidence.

Victims waste time at work and home building a defense against the abuse, politicking for support, and just running scenarios in their minds trying to form a corrective plan of action. Behaviors such as these interfere with productivity and employee motivation and eventually leave the employee with a sense of diminished self-efficacy and self-worth.

The general self-efficacy scale (GSE) created by Schwarzer and Jerusalem (1995) is a great scale to measure how confident employees feel about solving problems and setting goals. The scale may be used as a self-assessment or as an aggregate assessment of employee attitudes and beliefs about self-efficacy. While some of the data may reveal personality traits, a qualitative analysis may reveal that there are factors that decrease self-efficacy, as in the case of toxic workplace cultures.

Rating Scale: 1 = Not at all true 2 = Hardly true 3 = Moderately true 4 = Exactly true

1. I can always manage to solve difficult problems if I try hard enough.
2. If someone opposes me, I can find the means and ways to get what I want.
3. It is easy for me to stick to my aims and accomplish my goals.

4. I am confident that I could deal efficiently with unexpected events.
5. Thanks to my resourcefulness, I know how to handle unforeseen situations.
6. I can solve most problems if I invest the necessary effort.
7. I can remain calm when facing difficulties because I can rely on my coping abilities.
8. When I am confronted with a problem, I can usually find several solutions.
9. If I am in trouble, I can usually think of a solution.
10. I can usually handle whatever comes my way.

Scoring: Add up all responses to a sum score. The range is from 10 to 40 points, with the higher score indicating a higher self-efficacy.

Additionally, innovation in the workplace suffers because creative energies are redirected to meet unmet needs and to protect marginalized victims. Victims are known to create silo mentalities where information and resources are hidden to reduce the chance of interference from the bully. Silo mentalities are behaviors that are great time wasters for other more productive teams because of the restricted communication that it creates between departments, divisions, and partnerships.

Bystanders comprise the largest percentage of the workforce when it comes to the unjust destruction and rantings of the bully. Bystanders see the injustice that occurs when bullies are present in the workplace, and they often begin to distrust the organizational culture and purpose. After all, bullies are sometimes rewarded for their behavior, promoted, or ignored and left to operate as the status quo. A reward process based on bullying creates a misguided blueprint for otherwise mission-driven employees to follow in their efforts to climb a rather explosive ladder to the top. It is important to realize that bystanders are the organization's voice and will reveal the firm's actual level of organizational wellness to potential candidates, customers, vendors, and competing industries.

Another bully impact is the failure to communicate. When triads exist, otherwise stable employees begin to use dysfunctional methods to communicate everyday processes at work. In his Friday Talk News release, Dr. Dennis O'Grady (2015) clarifies the role of servant leadership, which is to control your mood so that you can fully exhibit your servant-leader character.[4] Within the bully triad, important components of effective communication are missing, and Dr. O'Grady lists eight select features of effective communication that must be a part of servant leadership and the culture of every healthy organization:

- *Respect.* Respect for others is shown by acknowledging their value as human beings.
- *Empathy.* Empathy leads to trust and creates strong bonds between people.
- *Lack of blame.* Lack of blame is the ability not to become defensive and willingness to admit mistakes with a focus on correcting the problem, not the person.
- *Humility.* Humility is a lack of arrogance. Humility means one does not think less of themselves—they just think more of others.
- *Emotional mastery.* Emotional mastery is, most importantly, the ability to control anger. Emotional mastery requires remaining calm, not berating others, controlling anxiety, and reflecting before acting.
- *Responsibility.* Responsibility is accepting ownership by being accountable.
- *Self-confidence.* Self-confidence is feeling equal to others, even when others may be in a position of formal power. Self-confident people build self-confidence in others and, in the process, are not threatened by doing so. Rather, they find growth within themselves.

- *Courage.* Courage is the willingness to take risk. Courageous people are sometimes known to ask forgiveness rather than permission. They are willing to try even though they may fail. They overcome obstacles, and their courage inspires others to change.

These select elements of effective communication are interpersonal and intrapersonal communication. However, organizations that embed these elements into managerial communication, policies, and procedures; organizational standards; and daily memos will see their efforts and strategies for healing the organization realized sooner.

Addressing the unmet needs of the triad that has developed because of workplace bullying will require a closer look at the functions of management and the organization's culture. Assessing the skills and competencies of the triad and fully rewarding these gifts by properly utilizing employee talent are also essential starting points for leveling power differentials in organizations. Also, truly listening to justice issues in the workplace and finding triggers for the unwanted behaviors of the triad will help the bully, the victim, and the bystander and stabilize organizational wellness.

An Organizational Approach to Workplace Bullying does not address the bully who brings weapons into the workplace to do harm because the legal system has provided a clear correctional system for dealing with the extreme violence and danger that these individuals present. Instead, *An Organizational Approach to Workplace Bullying* will help managers screen for and deactivate the tendency for bullies to create havoc and mayhem in the workplace by addressing the unmet needs of the workplace bully triad. In addition, *An Organizational Approach to Workplace Bullying* will help leaders assess the workplace environment to decide if certain norms may exist in the organization that helps promote future workplace bullies and distressed victims, and bystanders.

7

References

1. Colorado Bully Prevention Initiative. (2021). Bulling prevention resource guide. The Colorado Trust Foundation.

2. Dzurec, Laura Cox, PhD., P.M.H.C.N.S.-B.C., Kennison, Monica, EdD., R.N., & Albataineh, R., B.S.N. (2014). Unacknowledged threats proffered "in a manner of speaking": Recognizing workplace bullying as shaming. *Journal of Nursing Scholarship, 46*(4), 281-91.

3. Emdad, R., Alipour, A., Hagberg, J., & Jensen, I. B. (2013). The impact of bystanding to workplace bullying on symptoms of depression among women and men in industry in Sweden: An empirical and theoretical longitudinal study. *International Archives of Occupational and Environmental Health, 86*(6), 709-16.

4. O'Grady, D., (2021). What being a leader means: The role model for servant leadership. Retrieved from http://www.drogrady.com/.

5. Schwarzer, R., & Jerusalem, M. (1995). Generalized Self-Efficacy scale. In J. Weinman, S. Wright, & M. Johnston, Measures in health psychology: A user's portfolio. Causal and control beliefs (pp. 35-37). Windsor, UK: NFER-NELSON.

CHAPTER 2

Workplace Bully Triad Triage

It takes time to change a healthy organizational culture into a toxic workplace, and it will take time to create functioning teams that can collaborate and trust again. Therefore, the workplace bully triad triage is a process where emergency measures are implemented while long-term corrections are made to prevent future bully events. There are data collection systems that will reveal patterns that can be flagged for further analysis. For example, records that are based on accident and injury or absenteeism and poor employee satisfaction survey participation or results may be examined for trends.

Emergency measures might include revision of employee hiring and screening practices to prevent hiring employees with a record of workplace bullying. Reviewing absenteeism and accident and injury records may reveal patterns of dysfunction and areas where unreported bully events have occurred. Also, assessing the culture and conducting needs assessments will reveal where the most fragile areas of the workplace are located. These actions will help formulate an emergency plan to avoid knee-jerk reactions and give time for long-term solutions that can be explored rationally and with real-world, cost-effective measures. It would be essential to include employees in the process and to encourage ideas and suggestions.

To find a bully rather than create one, just look at the previous history and references of candidates and look for successful trends and top performance awards. A good way to determine if the candidate may have tendencies toward bullying would be to ask potential candidates to describe how and why they achieved these accolades. The descriptors they use may fit the I-type Instigator core traits of negative talkers developed by Dr. Dennis O'Grady (2014), such as *Winning Is Everything* or arrogantly omitting any collaborative work.[1] Understanding the character traits and communication styles of most workplace bullies would be a great addition to organizational screening processes as human resource specialists look for individuals who are the best fit for the organization. Communication consultants are also great to include as part of the assessment team because the evaluation will be based on an analysis that is free of organizational memories.

Also, candidates with short work histories or failure to develop within the organization may indicate that a person has been a member of a bully triad in the past. It is essential that during the screening process, questions are presented to explore the candidate's opinions and ideas or experience with workplace bullies. Often, members of previous bully triads consist of individuals who have tried to survive toxic workplaces, and bringing them into your organization may involve a time of healing so that the employee can learn to trust again and relinquish unhealthy coping mechanisms. Workplace bullying is common, and finding elements of past triads in new employees may help managers develop new employee orientation programs that include a triage area for support and clarification of acceptable behaviors and values.

Just like any quality or assessment process, new information may arise that indicates an area of neglect or mismanagement. Administrators are often surprised to find that there are hidden stories of neglect and abuse within healthy bottom-line and financial ratios. These stories may include actions that are not representative of the mission and values of the organization but, instead, may be the actions of desperate teams trying to exist in a toxic environment. It will be important to avoid judgment and reprimand during the assessment stage and wait for all the information to emerge concerning the true state of the organizational culture. The following diagram illustrates the assessment process. Workplace bully triad triage begins with a cultural assessment of your organization, followed by a needs assessment, and then an ongoing plan for change and support. Following a systematic process to produce a bully-free environment requires specific knowledge about your workplace and a desire for change.

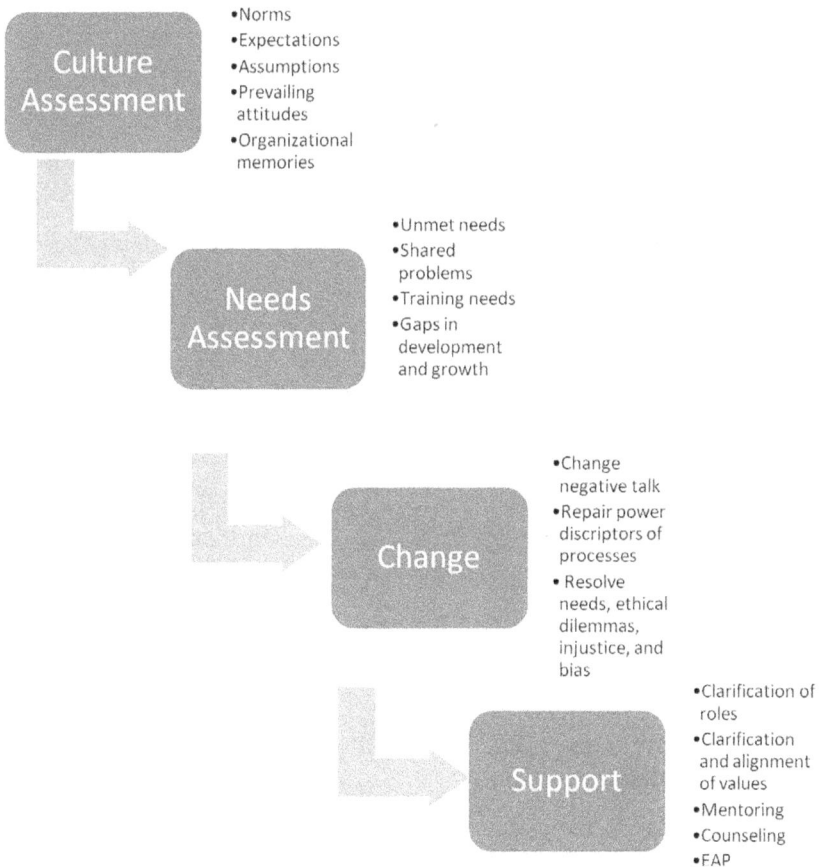

Culture Assessment
- Norms
- Expectations
- Assumptions
- Prevailing attitudes
- Organizational memories

Needs Assessment
- Unmet needs
- Shared problems
- Training needs
- Gaps in development and growth

Change
- Change negative talk
- Repair power discriptors of processes
- Resolve needs, ethical dilemmas, injustice, and bias

Support
- Clarification of roles
- Clarification and alignment of values
- Mentoring
- Counseling
- FAP

A healthy organizational culture will expose bullies and the practices that foster their rise to power. Assessing organizational culture to pinpoint the breeding factors for workplace bullies is an essential first step. According to Cameron and Quinn (2011), the foundation for workplace culture is derived from both sociological and archeological functions.[2] How an organizational culture is defined can be the starting point for the revision of existing standards and policies and procedures of the workplace. These may encompass values, assumptions, expectations, and the names or definitions that are assigned to members, groups, and subcultures. Organizational culture determines organizational performance consistently through the lean times as well as through times of excess, and the culture reflects the level of good in prevailing attitudes, organizational memories, and norms of the organization.[3] The organizational culture consists of more than the mission and values statements; however, a good starting point for establishing the desired organizational behaviors, norms, beliefs, symbols, brands, and future mindfulness is to identify the acerbic nature of developing bully triads quickly.

Organizational culture assessments reveal competing values and expose dominant frameworks that organize the workplace. Assessing the organization for competing values and dominant frameworks is a good starting point to determine how teams collaborate, create, control, and compete.[3] As culture types emerge from these assessments,; managers should then begin the screening process for common practices and even vocabulary that fosters a negative power balance throughout the workplace.[4] Depending upon the organizational structure, the culture type may be limited, but if abuse of power is embedded in the dominant framework, workplace bullies will begin to thrive.

There are many organizational assessments to choose that will help leaders look for trends in the organization that seems to be the driver for burnout and stress in the workplace. For example, the organizational culture assessment instrument (OCAI) is easy to score and examines six essential dimensions of workplace culture and generates a score for how managers of the organization view the organization now and the direction that they would like to see the organization take in the next five years.[3] Surveying line staff and middle managers will also broaden the scope of the assessment to include important elements of the culture that may be part of assumptions and norms of subcultures within the organization.

Another type of organizational assessment is a needs assessment survey that seeks to identify unmet needs and common or shared problems. Needs assessment surveys can be designed to survey for important needs of the workplace, wellness preferences and training, and development needs. Aggregate data analysis may show where resources have been manipulated or distributed unevenly and could reveal another area of workplace culture that may harbor bullies. Understanding the needs of the entire organization may help leaders identify ethical dilemmas and justice issues, as well as make sure that administrators are addressing the most important problems of all groups and subgroups.

Examining workplace culture and conducting needs assessment surveys will lessen blaming and finger-pointing because the surveys identify problems in an objective manner where managers may be less biased in the analysis of the data and reformulate the areas that seem to breed bully-like behaviors.[3] However, it is important to examine assessments and surveys individually to make sure that the data collection methods do not add further dominance issues regarding language, disability, or cultural challenges.[5] Reducing negative communication and looking for practices that are framed to create dominance and shame will reduce the triggers that stimulate a bully's aggressive behavior.[5]

For areas of the workplace that have been identified as fragile, it will be important to support those areas with mentors and employee assistance programs (EAP) and counseling. It will be essential to identify those employees who are at risk for violence, suicide, or organizational harm or those who are already in the job-exiting process. It is important to take threats of violence, organizational harm, and self-harm seriously and to take action and include outside agencies as the situation warrants. Employees who are looking to exit the organization should also be taken seriously and given a chance to relocate within the organization until the workplace is stabilized.

References

1. Talk2ME (2021). The cold communicator. Retrieved from http://www.drogrady.com/484/dealing-with-difficult-people-the-cold-communicator/

2. Cameron, K., & R., Quinn (2008). OCAI. Retrieved from http://www.google.com/url?sa=t&rct=j&q=&esrc=s&source=web&cd=2&ved=0sCC4QFjAB&url=http%3A%2F%2Fwww.uiowa.edu%2F~nrcfcp%2Fdmcrc%2Fdocuments%2Focai.doc&ei=N6KDVJeWL5KNyATp44DACQ&usg=AFQjCNFE1JXVkjaB5y15aj-1Z8UIb6lc5w&bvm=bv.80642063,d.aWw

3. Cameron K., and R. Quinn (2011). Diagnosing organizational culture. San Francisco CA: John Wiley and Sons, Inc.

4. Geller, S., (2014). Are you a workplace bully? Professional Safety (Jan. 14).

5. International Society for Performance Improvement. (2021). Handbook of improving performance in the workplace. San Francisco, CA: Pfeiffer/Wiley

CHAPTER 3

Examining Organizational Culture

In an effort to avoid lawsuits and low employee morale, managers encourage victims and bystanders to see the bullying situation as never being their fault.[1] However, if bullying is fostered by unhealthy organizational environments and toxic workplaces, then the very existence of the bully triad is a system problem and not necessarily an individual employee bully problem. The bully triad, which consists of the bully, the victim and the bystander may also consist of many members and actors who struggle to gain support and may position themselves and others to gain power in unhealthy outgroups and subgroups.

Organizational wellness requires support from the top down, especially when it comes to change that focuses on supportive relationships, feedback, and conflict resolution. In a bully triad, members switch roles and often learn the dysfunctional responses that work during a bully event. Seeing the bully triad as group in need of assessment, care, and realignment will help everyone to see the problem holistically. When bully triads exist, it should be a signal that there may be problems in more than one area and in more than one system. It should be a top-down process beginning with evaluating the mission, leadership, and the policy and procedures.

Micromanaging the bully and making the person an example is the wrong way to seek change in an already toxic work environment. Instead, providing assessment and support for the entire culture will lead to the identification of knowledge gaps that may lead to the development of the right training and creation of a mission-based cultural change.

These efforts should include the managers and supervisors because certain managerial competencies may actually dissolve the potential for bully triads to exist in the future (Cameron & Quinn, 2011).[2] For example, an administrator has two directors who have opposing views on a subject. They begin to clash, and it escalates negative behaviors. When one director reports the other director as being difficult, the administrator tells the director to confront the other director until something is worked out. The loyal director feels favored and sees the situation as an opportunity to use delegated power of authority to confront the other director in a hostile and abrupt manner. The situation resulted in both directors being viewed as difficult, bullish, and at a standoff regarding the immediate issue. However, both directors eventually identified themselves as victims of the system.

Who was the bully in the organizational memory or situation? Was the administrator the bully and just delegated his need to confront, or was the director a bully who was told to engage the other director? Depending on how bullying was defined, the other director could also be considered a bully because of the approach and the need to stand ground to protect or represent others. Perhaps, the chosen method to communicate would be a round table with all three members present to discuss the issue, which would have been a more participatory leadership style. Other thoughts to consider are the bystanders and the positioning regarding justice issues, the misuse of power, and the individuals affected by the toxic decision-making. Bully events that occur at the director level are carefully observed by lower-level management and staff. Depending on how these events are managed, director conflict may also negatively influence the workplace.

Policies and procedures must apply to everyone, and directors and managers must be held to a higher standard of conduct. Leaders work in groups, follow organizational pursuits, and participate in community projects and research. Leaders have a special responsibility to act ethically because of the influence that they have on others. Ethical behavior is central for top management because leaders help establish and reinforce organizational values, resource allocation, and the protection of the marginalized. Leaders are frontline staff and interact with many different agencies that follow their leadership, which compels directors and managers to pay close attention to the justice needs of their followers. Mistakes are made, and how mistakes are corrected may determine the lasting impact a mistake might have on the mission and values of the organization, brand image, and culture. Behavior and character are important factors to examine when it comes to organizational ethics, and desired behaviors and character may be learned through training, practice, and accountability. Leaders are called upon to reflect on their values, to avoid burnout, and to continually grow their knowledge and skills and competencies concerning technical skills and the soft skills needed to coexist.

In the story above, how can we determine if the organizational memory was a case of bullying? Unless bullying was defined and named in all its degrees, the conflict would probably be classified as inappropriate behavior until the problem escalated.[1] Unless organizations define bullying and all possible degrees in risk management policies, acts of bullying may go unnoticed until these acts escalate to workplace violence.[3] Labeling bullying must be managed by the entire team. The project may need diversity and inclusion consultants to overcome specific problems. For example, leaders and employees need to respect any pronoun preferences or name change or gender change that may occur in the workforce. Remembering names is difficult for some; however, changes that occur must be respected. Diversity and inclusion consultants may be able to help, and there are applications for helping managers and leaders remember names, name changes, and pronoun preferences. Respect for gender identity and orientation is just one example of where a situation may lead to bullying or persons being marginalized if certain choices are not respected.

In workplace environments where conflicts are allowed to develop to unpredictable levels, the workplace begins to resemble a training ground for terrorists where cognitive restructuring begins to distort values of the bully triad and may mask motives and agendas. For example, Bandura (1999) stated that immoral acts can be considered acceptable with cognitive reconstruction and reorganization of individual morals and values that justify the morality of affiliated group action. By utilitarian standards, the suffering that is created by terrorism is outweighed by the unjust acts of others. Although terrorists are considered victims of moral hijacking, as they have lost a part of their original identity, Bandura states that terrorism is a conscious and deliberate act (Bandura, 1999).

When members of the bully triad understand the definition and degrees of bullying, inappropriate workplace behaviors are screened or filtered through an agreed-upon framework or definition for bullying and a duty to warn prevails when defined bully acts trigger a threat assessment.[3] The first step in defining organizational bullying is to examine the mission and values of the organization. Within the organizational system of beliefs, philosophical priorities emerge that define the strategic plan and all other aspects of the functions of management.[4] In the purified state, without the pressure and stressors of the toxic bully triad, a mutual sense of rightness, trust, and dignity surround the vision of the organization. With a clear definition of bullying in mind, would the most common acts of the bully triad listed below be a part of the mission and vision of any successful organization?

- Silo thinking
- Gatekeepers of knowledge and future plans
- Sequestered resources or biased distribution of basic operational needs
- Micromanagement and negative communication

- Diminished or unfair distribution of rewards and recognition
- Lack of development and training withheld from certain individuals or groups
- Employees assigned to work that is demeaning or beyond their qualifications
- Unfair reward and recognition programs
- Discrimination
- Lack of diversity and inclusion
- Development of toxic outgroups and subgroups
- Delayed acceptance of diversity in the workplace (minority groups must prove their worth)
- Biased performance appraisals
- Impossible goals and targets set for certain individuals or groups

Obviously, CEOs and directors would not consider these acts as part of the mission and values of the organization, but everyone below these ranks may disagree. Perhaps it is in the pristine reports that are filtered up through the chain of command, who only focus on the final results, that misleads the higher-level executives to believe that the workplace culture is impeccable.

However, some of the first signs of a toxic culture are absenteeism, accident and injury, and poor retention. The next signs that a bully triad exists involve distrust, reduced loyalty, employee satisfaction decline, and finally, reduced quality, product defect, and poor productivity. In general, managers look for multiple causes for these declines, such as issues with an employee's medical or mental health. When, in reality, the problem may be a declining workplace culture. Next, managers start to examine the skills and competencies of their next line supervisors and invest in the next best training packages; however, if these supervisors are not trained to deal with bully triads, the situation may go unrecognized. When bullying is left unidentified or without definition, common acts of the bully triad will then continue to tarnish the organizational mission and value statement.

It is important to see the bully triad as a system problem and not caused by individual outliers of the organization. Bully triads exist because there is something wrong with the norms and ways of the workplace culture and the subcultures that exist. Even if a bully event was resolved, it would not take long for another bully event to occur because the way of conducting business has not changed. Systems are powerful and can provide a sense of rightness and justice, or they can perpetuate toxic behaviors and bully events that bog down operations. But systems that exist to standardize or to create processes that can measure workplace culture shifts are the best preventative measure to keep new bully triads from forming.

Organizational change toward healthy cultures may include the revision of policies and procedures, reward and recognition programs, job descriptions, orientation, training, and annual training, which should readdress the mission and values of the organization while declaring the organizational definition of bullying. Without an organizational definition of bullying and all its degrees, cognitive reconstruction occurs within the workplace environment that may justify all the dysfunctional behaviors of the bully triad until a devastating violent act occurs. Policies and procedures, job descriptions, and annual training should address the organizational definition of bullying so that bullying is considered abnormal or at least recognized as soon as it occurs.

Labeling and defining bullying provides relief to managers and leaders because the process becomes more objective and steps can be developed as to the next step for counseling or training of the individual or group involved. Also, labeling and defining organizational bullying should reduce the leader's conscious and unconscious bias regarding the issue. It is important to note that the labels for bullying may be different in different industries, divisions or departments. Looking at how other risks and threats are managed in the industry or organization may provide a template for a detailed strategy and plan of correction for workplace bullying.

References

1. Sandvik, P., (2013). *Adult bullying.* St. Louis, MO: ORCM Academic Press.
2. Cameron & Quinn, (2011). *Diagnosing and changing organizational culture.* San Francisco, CA. Jossey-Bass.
3. Richard, M., Emener, W., & Hutchinson, W., (2009*). Employee assistance programs.* Springfield, Ill: Thomas Books.
4. Bandura, A., (1999). Mechanisms of moral disengagement in terrorism. In W. Reich (Ed.) *Origins of terrorism: Psychologies, ideologies, theologies, stated of mind* (pp.161-199). Cambridge: Cambridge University Press.
5. Pearce, J., & Robinson, R., (2007). *Strategic management.* New York, NY. : McGraw-Hill/Irwin

CHAPTER 4

Assessment of the Bully Triad

Several things have been suggested to improve workplace wellness when dealing with the bully triad. For example, an organizational culture assessment was suggested, which is a good starting point for understanding the dominant characteristics, norms, leadership, and organizational memories and successes of the various subcultures within the organization. A needs assessment is another form of evaluation to determine workplace wellness because it measures the gaps between current conditions and optimal desires or outcomes for occupational wellness. Analysis and comparison of these two assessments often reveal uneven power differentials and unfair discrimination in resource allocation, which is frequently the modus operandi of the bully triad.

Analyzing the environment will help define the depth of the bully triad and the probable course of what may seem like a myriad of organizational system problems. The next suggestion involves examining the mission and values of the organization to establish a filter for defining bullying and all its degrees. The bully triad is a system problem and should be treated in the same way that other major organizational problems are managed. For example, systems that have run amok find alignment with total quality management and performance improvement initiatives. Quality assurance initiatives mean measurement and defining everything that is out of compliance so that performance improvement processes can reveal the embedded issues of the bully triad.

Frequently, when bully triads are operating, top managers struggle between the need to maintain the status quo and the need to repair or change the organizational culture to eliminate embedded bully triads. Concerns about top leadership exiting during change or operations bogging down because of policy changes or employee resistance to change are very real and difficult scenarios to face. Therefore, it is important to avoid changing everything at once. The needs and cultural assessments will reveal the top concerns to be addressed. Treating each major concern as an incremental organizational culture change project to be addressed individually will help keep objectives clear. Intuitively, top managers know that healthy organizational cultures are beneficial and more attractive to investors and the industry. Also, when healthy organizational cultures embrace change, they become more productive, creative, and innovative. Conducting a cost-benefit analysis for each incremental organizational culture change project will help validate intuition, attitudes and beliefs, and change through measurement.

In order to define the desirability of each organizational change project, it will be important to be able to measure both tangible and intangible benefits using a common unit of measurement such as money. For example, if interdepartmental communication was identified as the problem because of the dynamics of the bully triad, measuring employee turnover for each department, customer dissatisfaction, the cost of missed deadlines, and even absenteeism and accidents and illnesses may justify the organizational change project. It is also essential to look ahead and evaluate the future cost of poor communication using the discounted value or future value of a dollar available in five years if the decision was made to maintain the status quo.

The cost-benefit analysis should maintain consistency throughout each incremental organizational culture change project so that a comparison is always made between the differences of *with* versus *without comparison*. The question is how to measure the money saved by moving forward with incremental organizational culture change projects. Creating a portfolio for the process of the change results may help reduce the intimidating nature of change and improve employee buy in. Cost-benefit analyses are common in organizations to help top leaders decide how and when to spend funds to improve various market and operational needs. Actually, going through the process of placing a dollar value on the negative impact of bully triads within the organization gives the situation priority status because the losses experienced by organizational bully triads are identified and in a common language that everyone can understand.

Even though there is a high incidence of bullying in management teams and within groups of professional knowledge workers, their skills and competencies are very valuable to organizational success and brand image. It is not practical to scrap an entire workforce just because, operationally, the organization has created a toxic out-of-compliance workplace. Rather, it makes more sense to measure the problem, analyze the problem, and create a plan of action to change declining workplace wellness and dysfunctional systems. According to Kinicki and Kreitner (2006), when dealing with organizational problems, it is important to find a change model that provides sustained results rather than quick-fix solutions.[1] Taking the time to assess the culture, environment, and needs of the workplace will be well worth the effort because the process will reveal the internal forces for change, and it will reveal the salvageable good in the workplace bully triad.

What possible good can be gleaned from the bully triad? We can assume that members of the bully triad are valuable employees; otherwise, management would have already found ways to facilitate the exiting process. Much like autoimmune diseases that take perfectly good immune systems and begin attacking healthy systems in the body, a dysfunctional bully triad system will use the same skills and competencies that they are famously known for to navigate, survive, and attack other triad members. Using these skills to sell out each member of the bully triad, members of the triad will inevitably find ways to justify their stance unless they are given the opportunity for self-assessment and growth.[2]

There are numerous self-assessments for workplace behavioral assessment. Adult behavioral measurement instruments can be found at Buros Test Center, the CDC,[4] APA Testing Center,[5] and many other management consultant firms. Finding a self-assessment for specific workplace groups may take some research because it is important for the test to include the scoring information, and the information must be user-friendly for self-assessment. Additionally, it would be important to have the ability to mine valid and reliable aggregate data from the self-assessments to further facilitate analysis of organizational workplace wellness.

Another type of assessment that might be useful is to measure the ethical climate in your organization. Self-assessment that involves ethical considerations evaluates choices to act as being ethical or unethical, especially when compared with industry norms for acceptable behavior. Baird and Niacaris (2010) developed an Ethical Lens Inventory where personal expectations and behaviors are listed as "being included, being respected and respecting ourselves." The assessment evaluates according to individual values and personal motivation.[3] Ethical assessments may also provide aggregate data that may contribute to organizational and cultural assessment findings.

Diversity and inclusion attitudes and beliefs are another assessment to consider to determine how outgroups are managing the barriers that might exist for opportunity and development, access to the basic necessities of the workplace, and relationship-centered social groups across cultures. It is fairly easy to find surveys that are valid and reliable to give to employees to evaluate attitudes and beliefs about diversity and inclusion in the workplace. Northouse (2018) provides wonderful tools for assessment and for leadership to evaluate and define diversity and inclusion in terms such as trust, feeling safe, and accepted in the workplace.

Rubrics are another way to evaluate the signs and symptoms of the bully triad, and rubrics can be specifically designed for the organization. The benefit of a rubric method of assessment is that it captures the information from previous assessments to create assessments that are relevant to current conditions in the organization. Using only relevant rubrics may create productive conversations, and the information can be used to validate the depth and intensity of different bully triad scenarios. Interestingly, as educational programs evolve from all these assessments, rubrics can be used to objectively measure visible signs of learning, growth, and acceptance of workplace wellness initiatives. The rubric examples in the section below are somewhat generic in content, but it is easy to see how the rubric type of assessment could help the bully triad organize its position and stance concerning each category of the bully triad. It is possible that members may identify with more than one category of the triad depending on the length of time the triad has operated without intervention.

Through assessment, top leaders know what they do not want concerning organizational culture, but do they know what they want at the early stages of incremental organizational culture change? Going back to the mission and values of the organization and studying and reflecting on the *with* versus *without comparison* of healthy incremental organizational culture change is extremely important. If the organizational belief is that employees are the organization's greatest assets, how did the bully triad change the belief to one of disrespect? Do the various bully triads within the organization truly believe that their coworkers are the organization's best asset? Is there a common understanding concerning the value of each employee, or is there a general disrespect for other employees, cross divisions, and subcultures within the organization? The behaviors and artifacts of the organization create organizational stories, and if these stories are not reflective of the organizational culture or memories desired, the assessments mentioned in *An Organizational Approach to Workplace Bullying* will reveal why a disparity exists.

References

1. Kinicki & Kreitner (2006). *Organizational behavior.* New York, NY: McGraw-Hill/Irwin.
2. Patterson, K., Grenny, J., McMillian, Switzler, A., (2002). *Crucial conversations.* New York, NY. McGraw-Hill.
3. Baird, C., & Niacaris, J., (2010). *The person-in-community.* Denver, CO: Ethics Game Press.
4. Buros Center for Testing (2021). Clearinghouse. Retrieved from http://buros.org/clearinghouse
   CDC (2014). Violence prevention. Retrieved from http://www.cdc.gov/violenceprevention/pub/measuring_bullying.html
5. APA Testing Centers (2021). Retrieved from http://www.apa.org/search.aspx?query=tests

Triad Self-Assessment Rubrics

In the following rubrics, the triad is separated into their individual roles at the time of assessment. The self-assessments can be taken privately with the option for sharing or asking questions with a mediator or in a professional setting. The optimal rating and standard for bully-free environments would be a rating of three, with the rating of one being the lesser rating and three being a graded or incremental approach toward optimal criteria ratings.

Bully Assessment Rubric

Name _____Date _____

Optimal Criteria	1	2	3	Rating
I am able to work alone or in teams toward project completion.	I do the work alone. I do not trust the work of my coworkers.	Even if my coworkers help, I will have to spend a lot of time correcting their work.	I encourage coworkers to contribute, and I respect the work that they have provided.	
I applaud the talent of others and encourage their success.	I am the expert, and I am the most dedicated employee. I deserve the highest rewards.	My coworkers need my expertise, or they will fail in every aspect of the job. I should always get partial credit for the work.	I am able to mentor and step out of the way when others achieve success in their career or work.	
There are set guidelines and best practices in my organization, and they are to be respected.	I can get things done faster and better without the use of antiquated rules and guidelines.	Some guidelines do not make any sense, and I sabotage and undermine these standards frequently.	Guidelines and policies and procedures are in place for a reason, and if needed, I follow the chain of command to offer my suggestions.	
Collaboration and effective communication help organizations run smoothly.	I tend to be abrupt, and I will intimidate to get my way at work.	I attend meetings and remain civil until it is apparent that the members are wasting my time.	I am able to listen to all communicator types and contribute while being respectful.	

My organization is a top performer in the industry.	I push people beyond their limits without reward to meet unrealistic expectations and deadlines.	I only reward those employees who have followed my lead, and only these employees are given the opportunity to learn new skills and promote within the organization.	I value my coworkers and our leadership sets realistic goals and appropriate rewards and incentives without discrimination.	

Total _____

Victim Assessment Rubric

Name _____Date _____

Optimal Criteria	1	2	3	Rating
I feel that my creativity and innovation are protected and appreciated.	I am hypervigilant and dread coming to work.	Certain people at work make me question why I am here.	I feel needed and appreciated at work, and I share information and updates freely.	
I do not allow negative talkers to steal my peace of mind.	I am constantly thinking about being bullied or mistreated at work.	I rally support at work so that I can get my projects accepted on time.	I am able to communicate with different communicator styles effectively.	
I feel confident in the system that I will be rewarded for my work and contribution to the team.	I am afraid to offer my best effort because it will be minimized or my ideas will be stolen.	I am able to offer my best work, but I spend a considerable amount of time seeking support before offering the final work.	I include others in my creative processes and encourage others to contribute while still meeting deadlines.	
I feel confident at work, and I feel a strong sense of autonomy and have the ability to complete my work and reach my goals.	I am anxious and depressed, and I am absent frequently.	I have a good attendance, but I feel stressed and burned-out every day.	I do not experience unnecessary barriers at work, and I look forward to new challenges.	

I am excited about my work and career, and I feel comfortable with my work/life balance.	I feel overwhelmed concerning the unrealistic demands and goals set by others.	I can usually get the work done if I work on the weekends or take the work home to complete.	I have a great work/life balance, and I am able to pursue a healthy lifestyle from the entire spectrum of wellness.	

Total _____

Bystander Assessment Rubric

Name _____ Date _____

Optimal Criteria	1	2	3	Rating
I feel a sense of job security.	The rumors of bullying make me wonder if I am next.	My coworkers are seeking employment elsewhere, and I wonder if I should make plans to leave.	The organization is stable, and I feel that I can grow with the organization.	
My workplace meets and exceeds customer demands and satisfaction.	My productivity is down because coworkers are constantly talking about the bully or the victim.	Everyone is distracted and unable to focus on fulfilling customer needs because of the justice issues that the bully has created.	Everyone works together to achieve workplace goals, performance improvement, and plan for the future.	
I feel comfortable reporting to the chain of command for any issues that may arise.	I do not know who to trust anymore.	My coworkers avoid meetings, and little progress is made concerning resolving issues and problems.	Everyone has set roles and job functions and has a high level of trust in the reporting system.	
I am comfortable making long-range plans with my current workplace.	I am afraid to accept new professional development.	Many coworkers are overlooked for promotion or recognition because of sabotage and fear of retaliation from the bully.	I am able to learn new skills and apply them daily and build upon these competencies for future successes.	

I have a clear purpose and mission with the organization.	I feel that the mission and values of the organization are ignored.	Because the bully is allowed to operate unchecked, my coworkers are starting to ignore our mission and values.	The workplace is mission driven and focused on the values of the organization.	

Total _____

CHAPTER 5

An Organizational Approach to Workplace Bullying

An Organizational Approach to Workplace Bullying will involve more than just employee retraining and character building. The damage that has been done to the workplace culture by the bully triad has probably left every social system in the organization in disarray. The bully has been branded and has left a legacy of distrust, and other members of the triad may not be able to forget and move on so quickly. Remember, in the midst of the chaos, promotions were lost, opportunities were rerouted, and reputations were damaged. The bully triad must find the good in themselves and one another and move forward in forgiveness with a renewed focus on the organizational mission. In the current chapter, we will only focus on the conversion of the bully and examine the behaviors of the victim and the bystander in later chapters.

In the bully profile from *Chapter 1*, behaviors were identified that could lead to toxic environments and terrorist-like manipulation. Silo thinking was one of those fortress-building behaviors that often leads to sequestered resources and harboring of information, which may create territorial wars for distribution.[1] According to Raturi and Evans (2005), silo thinking promotes individuals or groups to focus on their own achievements and rewards rather than contributing to the organization's distinctive competencies.[2] Silo thinking is a symptom of an unhealthy organization and is often replaced by other management models that strive to be systems and mission oriented, which helps create an organization with healthier leadership and motivation.[3] Of course, preferred organizational leadership traits need to be clearly defined so that the bully could be given the opportunity to organize these leadership traits, with time, for reflection and reintegration into system thinking.

Abuse of power is another characteristic of bullies. If human resources properly screened for the characteristics of the bully prior to hiring and a bully ascended to power anyway, then the organization somehow created the bully. Perhaps the bully event was a result of scarce resources or built-in biases for dominance and control, discrimination, and injustice. Consider examining the organization for unusual obstacles concerning poor communication, role confusion, motivational incongruence, and ridiculous barriers to benefits and rewards.[4] It is important for leaders to consider the possibility of developing reward and recognition programs that meet every level of skill so that talents are recognized based on the individual and not on aggregate expectations. Some employees cannot compete or do not have the stamina to compete for rewards that are only designed for the elite employee.

Take a moment and return to the organizational cultural and needs assessments to see if these trends were reported by your employees. Employees that complain that certain processes for rewards, better jobs, or better hours and work environments are unjust, rigged, or politically motivated are probably stating the truth. Complaints or employee dissatisfaction are often not taken seriously but rather seen as just an expression of discontent from employees who have a sense of overentitlement. However, employee complaints that reoccur from survey to survey are revealing a system problem, such as misuse of power or bullying by management. Biased and discriminatory managerial decision-making is an abuse of power, and it can be subtle and found in the form of micromanagement to explosive coercion and intimidation. Structure the organizational culture differently by removing these barriers, clarifying roles, improving job descriptions, and by holding those in authority accountable for their actions and reactions regarding fairness.

Certain industries seem to cultivate aggressive communication because of the sheer emotional and physical difficulty of the job. Workers have never been given the tools to manage adrenaline, fear, anxiety, and failure, and as communication degrades in the workplace, the loudest and most fearful often rise to power. Communication training can help individuals understand their communication styles and those of their coworkers, and with skill development, employees and managers can learn to respectfully state their needs. According to Dr. O'Grady (2005), there are two different styles of communicators—Empathizers and Instigators.[5] Dr. O'Grady's New Insights Communication Inventory (NICI) can help workers determine if they are an Empathizer or Instigator communicator.[5] Strengths and faults can be found within each communicator style, and learning these factors can help bridge communication issues.

Investing in the failure of others sounds odd, but it is a characteristic behavior of the bully. History is full of people who wanted others to fail for personal gain. Behaviors such as these indicate that something is wrong with the emotional well-being of the employees or managers in the workplace. A sick workplace is created when the hierarchy of needs are not met, such as when the workplace is unstable or unsafe or social needs are ignored, when a lack of respect is the norm, and self-efficacy, fulfillment, and autonomy are missing in the workplace culture.[6] Workplace wellness programs are missing the mark when they only focus on the clinical and fitness needs of their employees. Health and wellness motivational theories all suggest that adherence and acceptance of the wellness programming depend upon the socialization of its participants.

The Vital Life Community wellness concept embraces the entire spectrum of wellness, such as the physical, intellectual, occupational, social, spiritual, nutritional, environmental, and emotional needs of each member of the organization, with the guiding principle being socialization. In a Vital Life Community organization, employees are provided opportunities to socialize with one another, form healthy relationships with others who have similar wellness goals, and develop an attitude of helping others. The benefits of having a workplace that knows how to socialize and support one another are too numerous to count. Blaming, incivility, and disrespect are greatly reduced in a Vital Life Community because employees are vested in the organization and in one another in healthy ways.

Blaming others for mistakes, missed production deadlines, or failure to meet performance improvement goals are symptoms of the toxic workplace. Bullies can effectively use blaming as they build evidence against victims to gain power. Fevre, Lewis, Robinson, and Jones (2012) found that managers and supervisors were often the sources for incivility and disrespect. Fevre et al. (2012) found that 40 percent of British employees experienced similar forms of treatment over a two-year period. The FARE score is a simple three-question survey to measure ill treatment in the workplace, and low scores indicate failing leadership and structure (Fevre et al., 2012). Training and policies to end ill-treatment in the workplace were the number one intervention recommended by these researchers. Interestingly, it was also recommended that global policies may not be enough, especially for managers and supervisors who feel that policies are only designed for subordinates (Fevre et al., 2012). Managers and supervisors should be held to a higher standard with policies that are relevant to their level of responsibility and power, and promotions and rewards should be based on the results of policy compliance and employee survey results.

FARE Score Questions:

- Where I work, the needs of the organization always come before the needs of people.
- Where I work, you have to compromise your principles.
- Where I work, people are treated as individuals.[6]

Undervaluing others in the workplace breeds discrimination, biases, and negative stereotypes. Rosenblum and Travis (2012) stated that education is the foundation to social change and that individuals must reflect on his or her beliefs about others.[7] In addition, it is important for employees to learn to value the master statuses that they occupy and become comfortable with their race, ethnicity, gender, social class, disability, and sexual orientation so that they can begin to value others.[7] Diversity and inclusion training is a great addition to managerial training because it leverages the strengths in a diverse workplace and highlights the benefits of professional relationships, innovation, and creativity. Also, diversity training is a great motivator for employees of all backgrounds because employees with diversity training become confident in their contributions, skills, and competencies and are respectful of all other employees. Diversity and inclusion training also helps uncover those policies and procedures that are unfair or inadequate concerning opportunities for employees from all backgrounds.

Shaming or humiliating others in the workplace is another bully behavior that can be difficult to identify because victims are often too ashamed to report personal episodes of harassment. Victims begin to believe the bully's shaming remarks and criticism, and publicly identifying shaming only increases the sense of diminished self.[8] However, building peace in the workplace begins with humiliation and harassment policies, and training in empathy, and identifying sociopathic or unacceptable behavior.[8] It is part of the naming process in the bully definition process so that shaming or humiliating attacks are identified so that these acts can be dealt with in a way that does not perpetuate the devaluing of others. Empathy training teaches employees to listen, to recognize the feelings of others, and to communicate an understanding of those feelings. Empathy training will help employees maintain their identity while participating with but also respecting the feelings of others. There are different empathy courses and valid and reliable surveys for empathy training on the market, but empathy training is definitely a way to build a compassionate workplace.

The bully as a disruptor or rule changer exists with the organization's blessing and is free to misuse power and add destructive abuse of anchors to the toxic mix. Managers or employees who are allowed to dismiss or change the rules are in the position of power because they have been granted unearned power.[9] Bullies have great skills for finding key personnel or anchors within an organization who may need support or favors. Creating indebtedness and dependency is one of the bully's insidious tools for manipulation. Because of the toxic relationship created by the bully, busy and overworked managers may look the other way when bullies misbehave. Bullies may even be seen as the organizational hero or even as an altruistic employee when they create these dependent relationships with their leaders. When in reality, the bully has just been granted unearned power in exchange for these special favors.

It is essential to maintain checks and balances for policy making and decision-making for all rules within the organizational structure. Transparency and congruency of rules from every level of the organization are critical. Policies are often in place and exist for years without being updated or checked for illicit changes or outdated content. Policies, procedures, and organizational rules degrade over time, and unless they are reviewed and approved by all groups, disruptors and rule changers can make hidden changes for personal gain.

Sabotaging team members and squelching creativity and innovation is a bully behavior too, and it might encompass passive behaviors to resistive behaviors. For example, a wellness program was launched in one organization, and upper management had agreed to participate and to role model a desire to be healthy and to make healthier lifestyle choices. A key member of the management team suddenly remembered how much she loved potato chips and placed bowls of packaged single-serving chips throughout her office. While she did not verbally denounce the wellness program, her action spoke volumes. And as a leader with influence, her passive voice mocked the program. The individual was bold in her actions, and because of her position and power, she knew that her boycotting actions would not be questioned by her superior. The entire wellness program becomes a work-around for those individuals who followed the boycotted wellness program until it had no value at all. Before an initiative is launched that involves a campus- or organization-wide change, it is essential to have commitment by top members. Programs that start at the top and filter down to the ranks below should also be monitored for support and loyalty. Teambuilding, trust, and interdependence can only occur when everyone who has power has a vested interest in fostering a healthy and productive group (Wheelan, 2005).

Claiming fame to visible projects is bully behavior that is based on lack and impoverishing others. By stealing success and the lion's share of opportunities for development, the bully ensures that others cannot possibly compete for success and fame. Falsely claiming rewards successfully is also a system problem because of poorly designed employee recognition programs that focus on individuals rather than teams or groups. Projects and special programs must provide fair access to all employees, and teams should be rewarded for their success in meeting objectives together. Collaborative team members emerge from well-defined goals and objectives, and creating well-defined goals and objectives provides a place for every member of the team.[2]

It is well-known that bullies criticize and create destruction in the workplace, and the methods and results that they use are too numerous to count or list. When the situation does not improve with specific training and the approaches listed throughout *An Organizational Approach to Workplace Bullying*, managers may be prudent to request that the bully seek professional help. Employee assistance programs (EAP) are a great place to start to give the bully a chance to voice injustices or false reports of bullying. It takes a lot of energy and vigilance to be a bully, and mental health issues may arise from both the successes and the failed attempts to bully. Any signs of emotional decline should be taken seriously. Psychometric testing and other approaches from mental health professionals may help narrow the issue and provide direction for treatment. Mental health issues may be short- or long-term and could be medically-based and, possibly, even become an issue of disability.[10]

Resources

1. Gleeson, B., (2013). The silo mentality: How to break down barriers. Retrieved from http://www.forbes.com/sites/brentgleeson/2013/10/02/the-silo-mentality-how-to-break-down-the-barriers/
2. Raturi A., & Evans, J., (2005). *Principles of operations management.* U.S.A.: Thomson/Southwestern
3. Studor, Q., (2003) *Hardwiring excellence.* Gulf Breeze, Fl.: Fire Starter Publishing
4. Kazén, M., & Kuhl, J. (2011). Directional discrepancy between implicit and explicit power motives is related to well-being among managers. *Motivation and Emotion, 35*(3), 317-327.
5. O'Grady, D., (2021). *Talk to me.* Dayton, Oh: New Insights.
6. Harder, H. (2014). Retention via the millennial hierarchy of workplace needs. Retrieved from http://heatherharderpr.com/2014/09/24/how-doing-good-helps-recruit-and-retain-millennials/
7. Fevre, R., Lewis, D., Robinson, A., & Jones, T. (2012). Insight into ill-treatment in the workplace: patterns, causes and solutions. *Contemporary Readings in Law and Social Justice, 4*(2), 245-277.
8. Cardiff University, (2014). Insight into ill-treatment in the British workplace. Retrieved from http://www.cardiff.ac.uk/socsi/insight/fare/index.html
9. Rosenblum, K., & Travis, T., (2012). *The meaning of difference.* New York, NY: McGraw-Hill.
10. Harper, J., (2013). Beyond bullying. Retrieved from http://www.psychologytoday.com/blog/beyond-bullying/201309/bullying-mobbing-and-the-role-shame
11. Wheeler, S., (2005). *Group process.* New York, NY: Allyn & Bacon/Pearson House.
12. Pinel, J., (2009). *Biopsychology.* New York, NY: Pearson Education Inc.

Conversion Chart for
Workplace Bully Behaviors

After Reviewing Possible Bully Behaviors,
Research Appropriate Training Programs to Support Reintegration.

Bully Behaviors	Reintegration Training	Skill Retention
Master at creating silos	Organize leaderships traits	Motivational leader
Abuser of power	Clarify roles and job descriptions	A just leader
Aggressive communication	Investigate Instigator/ Empathizer communication styles	Effective communicator
Invests in the failure of others	Survey for unmet needs or missed skills	Confident leader
Blames others	Survey for self-efficacy (GSE scale)	Committed leader
Undervalues others	Diversity training	Engagement leader
Shames others	Empathy training to reduce perfectionism, inadequacy perception, and power misuse	Empathizer leader
Disruptor / rule changer	Reaffirm policies/ procedures and guidelines	Performance improvement team member
Sabotages team creativity and innovation	Build interdependence and trust with team-building programs	Collaborative team member
Claiming fame and visible projects	Reevaluate employee recognition and reward programs for fairness, and shift the balance from individual to group success	Innovation leader
Criticizes and creates destruction	Identify prevailing values of the organization, and clarify the values and beliefs of the bully via psychometric testing	Compassionate leader

CHAPTER 6

Finding the Good in the Workplace Victim

It is not helpful to tell victims that they are not responsible for the toxic triad behavior or the bully's responses. Dismissing the victim's role in the situation may create barriers to important opportunities to negotiate and collaborate for workplace rights and privileges and for the entire triad to gain self-efficacy based on mutual respect and trust. Blaming only the bully, mob bullies, or leadership club bullies will create further silos or groups that just go underground with their behaviors and agendas. Naming the inappropriate behaviors of the entire triad and comparing the list to the mission and values of the organization will reveal the deficits in organizational training and development so that the organization may direct performance improvement toward a healthier and more functional workplace.

Workplace victims exhibit a wide range of behaviors and may even switch roles within the triad because they are on a frantic mission to find an approach that will work. Victims are trying to find an approach to manage bullying that will yield the best compromise concerning a situation that does not seem to have an immediate resolution. Victims are trying to maintain their commitment to work responsibilities, productivity, accuracy, and precision while defending personal honor and protection of goals and dreams.[1] The battleground is occurring at the expense of the organization and at the expense of each member of the organization. For management, the only behaviors that seem to gain the most attention are the bully's chaotic tirades, and once modeled, they will be repeated at least a thousand times by other members of the triad to capture that same attention.

According to research, catastrophizing the pain that is caused by the bully provides a sense of control for the victim. The storytelling that is created by the phenomenon contains a mixture of real and imagined injury and pain.[2] Therefore, victim reports of PTSD, burnout, stress, and anxiety are often met with some skepticism, especially with low-level bullying. Standardizing victim language on assessment surveys may help victims be more objective in revealing important details about incidents so that appropriate action may be taken by the organization.[3] Focusing on victim responses to psychological pain after bullying episodes concerning rumination, helplessness, and magnification may provide a better understanding of victim reports of bullying for the victim and the organization.[2]

A hesitancy to work synchronously or asynchronously is a victim avoidance behavior that is prevalent during bullying. Often there are enough checks and balances in the human resource manual where victims are hesitant to retaliate against bullying behaviors to the level that reveals their true anguish over lost workplace opportunities. Therefore, avoiding interaction with the bully may seem to be the less violent course of action. Avoidance may involve a reluctance to work on group projects and communicate and may be the dominant factor in increased absenteeism and turnover.[4] Of course, passive aggressive behaviors such as these can undermine an organization's operations and stall progress on projects, creativity, and innovation. Looking at avoidance issues as a system problem may be helpful because there are things that can be put in place to ensure that the victim has equal access to workplace opportunities during the cultural transformation of the organization to a healthier workplace. Creating processes to ensure transparency and authenticity of work teams can be designed to time-stamp individual effort for credit.

Some of the behaviors in the victim profile are indifference to promotion and development and issues with role clarity. These behaviors are not surprising because bullies are known for hijacking the victim's hard work, dedication, and rewards. Bullies also cherry-pick job descriptions and tasks so that their stolen gains are again more visible for possible rewards. It would make sense that the victim would become unsure about their position and role within the organization. Because when the bully is left unchecked for so long, even line managers may be unsure of job description assignment and responsibility. It is important for managers over triads to be familiar with each member's job description so that accurate job analysis can be accomplished for performance measurement and for safety.[5]

Fearful and restricted communication occurs when there is conflict and dysfunctional negotiation involving stifling one member's voice within the conflict. Whether it involves the bully using unequal power or creating toxic anchors for support, the victim becomes marginalized and unable to effectively communicate needs within the bully triad. Toxic and troublesome workplace scenarios often include negative and positive communicators, and when they are misunderstood, conflicts often occur.[6] Fearful and restricted communication is a typical response for victims, and to complicate matters, their opposite communicator type is often used by the bully.

Workers who understand their communication styles can work on maintaining the positive and productive characteristics of their communicator style while letting go of or changing negative communication blunders.[6] Just like other managerial dilemmas, correcting miscommunication, misuse of communication, and communication used to bully others will require assessment and development and training to increase healthy dialogues. According to Dr. O'Grady (2005), conflicting and negative communication results in negative communication, misunderstandings, and missed content within the message. Dr. O'Grady (2005) suggests six skills to create better communication. The first suggestion involves understanding your communicator style and then the style of your adversary so that there is an understanding of how each person is relating to the dialogue. The diagnosis of the communication types within the triad is a starting point for understanding the design and intention of the message before it is launched.[6] In addition, as communication improves and a better understanding of communicator types emerge, members can use more of the strengths of each communicator type to problem solve, negotiate, and communicate fairly.[6]

When a person is told no or is restricted from being his or her personal best or contributing at the level to which he or she is accustomed, autonomy diminishes, and self-confidence is damaged. According to Max DePree (2004), it is in our nature to seek belonging, contribution, and dedication in the workplace. For the bully triad, attempts to stabilize these needs are met with hostility because there is a lack of respect for personal or group contribution. Usually, disrespect is the case because of unfair recognition and rewards. It does not matter that the star manager is turning everything into gold if the rest of the team spends most of the time out of the spotlight. Eventually, the uneven distribution of attention will be sabotaged by members of the bully triad. DePree (2004) stated that respect for contributions involves bringing to the spotlight everyone's gifts at different times and in different ways.

Reduced self-efficacy and indecision are victim behaviors that come with a high price concerning procrastination and inaction. Normally, competent leaders and employees become despondent after just short periods of bully exposure. The self-efficacy scale (GSE) is a measure of personal beliefs concerning accomplishment and goal achievement. Questions in the GSE assessment measure difficulty in solving problems, perseverance, resourcefulness, and conflict resolution. The GSE assessment can be used for self-reflection and, on an aggregate level, for triad triage and rescue.

Victims are often uninterested in personal development or the development of others. Their entire focus is short-term and based on exiting. It is important to provide opportunities to engage the victim in the good that is occurring around them. Diversity training is a great way to refocus the victim from being self-centered to being focused on the community aspect of the workplace. Diversity training can be more than just exploring differences. Diversity training can help members of the triad examine competing values and threats.[7] Diversity training helps to map out expectations and builds a path for coping and managing differences within the workplace respectfully.

If the bully triad exists for any length of time, a sense of hopelessness will prevail, and hopeless attitudes will also be reflected in employee satisfaction surveys. A lack of empathy for others and the organization will seep into the organizational culture turning organization memories into negative events that will tarnish brand image over time. Empathy training increases understanding and builds trust during times of critical and negative periods in the organization. Empathy training fosters compassion and relationships that are based on trust and listening.[8]

It is common when access to resources and rewards are shut off, employees begin to work around issues by finding the least resistance to completion of tasks. However, the escape process causes decay of organizational policies and procedures and best practices. Policies are designed to free managers from having to make repetitive decisions because policies and procedures offer consistency and expectations concerning behavior and performance.[9] Therefore, it is essential that the policies and procedures are redefined and reaffirmed after bully triads disband to eliminate continued victim behaviors.

Hypervigilance and exiting teams are victim behaviors that are hard to manage because the environment feels unsafe and intimidating. Creating policies and clear expectations for a nonviolent and bully-free work environment are important steps to build trust again in the workplace. However, manager and leadership training that deals with the empowerment of all staff and appropriate conflict resolution will create a plan from the top down that support and brings life to those policies.[9] The goal is to build functional teams that collaborate and trust one another again.

PTSD and burnout are issues for the entire bully triad, and these issues are serious enough to warrant an evaluation concerning each member's personal agendas and intentions for possible harm. Holding grudges and sabotaging organizational property and innovation are just some of the warning signs that violence may be pending.[9] These warning signs or levels of anger or grief are often due to a loss of something that is felt as an entitlement because of hard work and dedication. Bullies without boundaries grab rewards and recognition without pause if the organizational system for rewarding employees is dysfunctional or unfair. Organizations must create employee recognition and rewards that are fair for everyone, and the focus must be shifted from individual rewards to group success. It is through the group's success that personal identity returns and self-efficacy grows within the collaborative environment.[10]

Sometimes, after a bully triad is dissolved, there are still feelings of shame and feeling that beliefs and values have been compromised along the way. Once compassionate leaders feel lost and disillusioned, it may be difficult to regain self-confidence and trust in themselves and others. Psychometric testing of beliefs and values can help employees find their center again and realize that the prevailing values of the organization have been realigned to their original state. A tangible process such as psychometric testing helps employees realize why they chose the organization as part of their life course and helps them find their passion again.

References

1. Rasool, F., Arzu, F., Hasan, A., Rafi, A., & Kashif, A. R. (2013). Workplace bullying and intention to leave: The moderating effect of the organizational commitment. *Information Management and Business Review, 5*(4), 175-180.

2. Karpinski, A. C., PhD., Dzurec, Laura C, PhD., P.M.H.C.N.S.-B.C., Fitzgerald, S. M., PhD., Bromley, Gail E, PhD., C.N.S., & Meyers, T. W., M.S.N. (2013). Examining the factor structure of the pain catastrophizing scale (PCS) as a measure of victim response to the psychological pain of subtle workplace bullying. *Journal of Nursing Measurement, 21*(2), 264-83.

3. Sullivan, M., Bishop, S., & Pivik, J., (1995). The pain catastrophizing scale: Development and Validation. Psychological assessment, 7, 524-532.

4. Casimir, G., McCormack, D., Djurkovic, N., & Nsubuga-Kyobe, A. (2012). Psychosomatic model of workplace bullying: Australian and Ugandan schoolteachers. *Employee Relations, 34*(4), 411-428.

5. Noe R., Hollenbeck, J., Gerhart B., & Wright P., (2010). *Human resource management.* New York, NY: McGraw-Hill/Erwin.

6. O'Grady, D., (2021). *Talk to me.* Dayton, Oh: New Insights.

7. DePree, M., (2004). *Leadership is an art.* New York, NY: Doubleday Publishing.

8. Marsiglia, F. & Kulis S., (2010). *Diversity oppression and change.* Chicago, Ill.: Lyceum Book, Inc.

9. Empathy Styles (2014). A fresh approach to management and leadership. Retrieved from http://www.empathystyles.com/freshapproachtomanagement.php.

10. Ivancevich, J., (2004). *Human resource management.* New York NY: McGraw/Hill.

11. Johnson, D., & Johnson, F., (2003). *Joining together.* New York, NY: Allyn Bacon.

Conversion Chart for
Workplace Victim Behaviors

After reviewing victim behaviors, research
appropriate training programs.

Victim Behaviors	Reintegration Training	Skill Retention
Hesitancy to work synchronously or asynchronously	Time-stamp work for authenticity to ensure credit until trust issues are resolved	Motivated leader
Unsure about position and role in the organization	Clarify roles and job descriptions	A just leader
Fearful and restricted communication	Investigate Instigator/ Empathizer communication styles	Effective communicator
Reduced autonomy and lack of confidence	Survey for unmet needs or missed skills	Confident leader
Reduced self-efficacy/ indecisive	Survey for self-efficacy (GSE scale)	Committed leader
Uninterested in the development of self or others	Diversity training	Engagement leader
Critical, negative, disgruntled worker	Empathy training to reduce perfectionism, inadequacy perception, and power misuse	Empathizer leader
Works around issues rather than maintaining best practices	Reaffirm policies/ procedures and guidelines	Performance improvement team member
Hypervigilance / exiting teams	Build interdependence and trust with team-building programs	Collaborative team member
PTSD and burnout issues	Reevaluate employee recognition and reward programs for fairness, and shift the balance from individual to group success	Innovation leader

Feels values and beliefs are compromised	Identify prevailing values of the organization, and clarify the values and beliefs of the victim via psychometric testing	Compassionate leader

CHAPTER 7

Finding the Good in the Workplace Bystander

Bystanders are a captive audience during times of bully and victim conflict, and bystanders often take sides during conflict or rally for support inappropriately through the development of unhealthy subcultures. Just like the analysis for the bully and the victim, these behaviors interfere with productivity, brand image, and employee and customer satisfaction. It is a false assumption that inappropriate bystander behaviors will disappear when the conflict between the bully and the victim is resolved. Like other members of the bully triad, bystanders can switch roles and become victims and, in worst-case scenarios, become bullies themselves. The maladaptive behaviors continue with the bully triad, and organizational memories will be tainted with feelings of insecurity and shame. Bystanders should also be included in reintegration and organizational training for a better workplace culture. It is also important to realize that bystanders are individuals and may require training that specifically addresses their needs in order for the bystander to be able to trust the workplace environment enough to let go of unhealthy communication and maladaptive behaviors.

When bystanders are quiet, there are usually underlying threats that keep individuals and groups from stepping up to help or report bullying and abuse. In the case of children who cannot speak for themselves, some bystanders may feel threatened or even benefit by not intervening and will only do so if there is a chance that others will report the abuse. Also, when bystanders are quiet and not involved in the abuse or bullying of adults or children, fear or uncertainty may be why. However, in the presence of a bully, the behavior exhibited by the victim and the bystander goes beyond apathy to fear-based. According to Dr. Albrecht (2012), there are five fears common to humans.

Fear Types:

(1) fear of extinction,
(2) fear of body mutilation or invasion,
(3) loss of autonomy,
(4) fear of separation, abandonment or rejection,
(5) ego-death or fear of humiliation, shame, or worthlessness.

Since bullying is a system problem, the diffusion of responsibility to not intervene or report bully behavior becomes rationalized because of the fears embedded in the culture. The fears that are created become unmet needs, which increases the feelings that the environment is not safe.

Nielsen and Finarsen (2013) found that bystanders do not have a high incidence of depression because they witness the bullying of others but that it is more likely that they have been bullied themselves. Interestingly, it was recommended that the bystander be the focus of future research in order to truly determine the cost of workplace bullying.[1] Emdad, Alipou, Hagberg, and Jensen (2013) found that rumors in the workplace that were based on negative gossip and inaccurate facts are prevalent during workplace bullying and that these rumors can lead to employee dissatisfaction, exit seeking, and future episodes of depression and job anxiety. According to these researchers, there are many categories of responses that can be felt by the bystander, thus bringing mental anguish for a full range of feelings and behaviors from guilt, to promoting retaliation, to internalizing the pain and suffering of others, and even to bargaining for relief from the drama.[2]

Whistle-blowing may not be considered an option for the bystander if he or she feels that the act may bring further threat or loss to workplace opportunities. The act of reporting a bullying event to defend the workplace may be avoided if whistle-blowing is perceived as being equal to or a greater threat to emotional well-being than doing nothing[3]. Moreover, avoidance behavior was also found when bystanders perceived the situation to be very serious even though the bullying act or victim response was viewed as having the potential of yielding a high personal cost[3]. Although most organizations use employee assistance programs (EAP) to counsel employees privately and mediate conflict between individuals, research has found that third-party channels for reporting bully triad behaviors are trusted by employees to be confidential and are used more frequently than those connected to the organization[3]. Third-party reporting channels for bullying events are particularly useful when there are many bystanders involved. Of course, the risk of using third-party reporting for whistle-blowing is the loss of organizational brand image and reputation.

Organizations spend a lot of time, effort, and resources marketing and communicating their brand image to the public; however, they miss the most important market segment, which is comprised of the employees in the everyday workplace. Employees give the best testimony that verifies that an organization is upholding the mission and values that they broadcast. Poor retention rates indicate that there is a problem with the organizational culture, and exiting staff often become walking billboards for stories of workplace abuse, mistreatment, and unjust employee performance improvement. Low response and poor attitudes reflected in employee satisfaction surveys are just the symptoms that a larger dysfunction is present and affecting emotional wellness in the workplace. Internal marketing to promote the realignment of corporate values is essential for organizations who are trying to heal bystanders and other members of the bully triad.

A return to the organization's mission and values is a priority when trying to redirect members of an unhealthy workplace back to the original goals and purpose of the organization. Throughout *An Organizational Approach to Workplace Bullying*, when bully triads exist, there has been a call for organizational change, which was followed by the need to change policies and procedures, implement just and fair rewards and recognition, and enhance clarification of roles and job descriptions. Changing the evaluating and controlling aspects of management to reflect these changes will produce a common viewpoint for employees and management to reestablish new norms, symbols, and icons in the workplace. Decreased involvement in social functions and efforts to build a collaborative environment will not disappear immediately, and the delay is mainly because of the cultural incompatibility that often exists during change.[4] In order to build a social climate of acceptance and camaraderie, there must be a great deal of commitment and dedication directed toward the change. Employee engagement occurs only after threats to security and psychological safety are resolved and belongingness, self-esteem, and autonomy return.

Bystander behaviors can be redirected toward positive outcomes once the organizational culture begins to change, and redirection may include ongoing training and workshops for diversity, empathy, communication, and leadership. In the case of the workplace, bystander intervention can only be positive when the organization is moving toward a consistent culture that supports organizational goals and purpose. Many psychological studies have revealed that bystanders will intervene and become potential helpers if the bullying event is an act that has been labeled as offensive.[5] Earlier in *An Organizational Approach to Workplace Bullying*, the importance of labeling inappropriate behaviors and acts of violence was explored to the point of basing job descriptions, performance reviews, and policies and procedures around these definitions. Education for the bystanders in the organization will reduce the anxiety of being a bystander and the stress to act, not act, or react in a given situation.[5]

Managers and administrators need to lift their gaze above the bullying event to determine the damage or aftermath of the event. For example, are employee survey ratings poor or perhaps avoided altogether? An analysis of the social environments in the workplace and participation rates in team-building and collaborative projects in the workplace will be another factor that might indicate that the organization has more bystanders than originally thought.

The bystander effect indicates that the more witnesses there are concerning an emergency or negative event, the less likely individuals will step forward and help.[6] When a bully is left unchecked, bystanders feel that their intervention would be too costly on a personal level or so insignificant to promote change, that the stress of remaining an apathetic bystander is considered a necessary tradeoff. The longer the situation goes without an organizational culture change, the more toxic and unstable the work environment will become.

When employees are treated as customers, a market environment develops concerning needs-based exchanges.[7] When work products are delivered as needed and without penalty or unnecessary conditions, loyalty, trust, motivation, performance, satisfaction, and psychological empowerment begin to grow. Organizations would never consider anything less for their external customers, and leaders would never allow one customer to bully another. In a hostile bully work environment, internal customers do not exist because employees are used as mere means to an end; therefore, there is a failure to thrive and a disinterest in the above commitment. Bystanders in a toxic environment will wait passively for instruction; however, in an environment that is bully-free, everyone is active and empowered to move toward greater efficiency.

References

1. Albrecht, D., (2012). The five fears we all share. Retrieved from https://www.psychologytoday.com/us/blog/brainsnacks/201203/the-only-5-fears-we-all-share

2. Nielsen, M. B., & Einarsen, S. (2013). Can observations of workplace bullying really make you depressed? A response to emdad et al. *International Archives of Occupational and environmental Health, 86*(6), 717-21.

3. Emdad, R., Alipour, A., Hagberg, J., & Jensen, I. B. (2013). The impact of bystanding to workplace bullying on symptoms of depression among women and men in industry in Sweden: An empirical and theoretical longitudinal study. *International Archives of Occupational and Environmental Health, 86*(6), 709-16.

4. Gao, J., Greenberg, R., & Wong-On-Wing, B. (2015). Whistleblowing Intentions of Lower-Level Employees: The Effect of Reporting Channel, Bystanders, and Wrongdoer Power Status. *Journal Of Business Ethics, 126*(1), 85-99.

5. Cameron K., & Quinn, R., (2011). *Diagnosing and changing organizational culture.* San Francisco, CA: Jossey-Bass.

6. McMahon, S. A. (2011). "Being in a Room with Like-Minded Men": An Exploratory Study of Men's Participation in a Bystander Intervention Program to Prevent Intimate Partner Violence. *Journal of Men's Studies, 19*(1), 3-18.

7. Greitemeyer, T. D. (2013). Rational bystanders. *British Journal Of Social Psychology, 52*(4), 773-780.

8. Qing yaorong chenguoliang, c. (2013). How internal marketing can cultivate Psychological empowerment and enhance employee performance. *Social Behavior & Personality: An International Journal, 41*(4), 529-537.

Conversion Chart for
Workplace Bystander Behaviors

After reviewing possible bystander behaviors, research appropriate training programs to support reintegration.

Bystander Behaviors	Reintegration Training	Skill Retention
Halo effect for employee satisfaction surveys—low response and poor attitudes	Resolve issues with the bully and the victim and begin values training and an internal marketing campaign to realign corporate values	Emotional wellness leader
Decreased involvement in social functions and efforts to build a collaborative environment	Create an environment of trust and safety by publishing and providing workshops to announce new policies and procedures to control negative workplace behaviors	Social wellness leader
Decreased creativity and focus	Provide workshops on burnout and stress at the workplace	Occupational wellness leader
Reduced autonomy and lack of confidence	Survey for unmet needs or missed skills	Confident leader
Reduced self-efficacy/ indecisive	Survey for self-efficacy (GSE scale)	Committed leader
Uninterested in the development of self or others	Diversity training	Engagement leader
Critical, negative, disgruntled worker	Empathy training to reduce perfectionism, inadequacy perception, and power misuse	Empathizer leader
Works around issues rather than maintaining best practices	Reaffirm policies/ procedures and organizational chart / structure guidelines	Performance improvement team member

Hypervigilance / exiting teams	Build interdependence and trust with team-building programs	Collaborative team member
Development of unhealthy subcultures	Leadership training to reduce silo thinking	Dedicated leader
Feels values and beliefs are compromised	Identify prevailing values of the organization and clarify the values and beliefs of the victim via psychometric testing	Compassionate leader

CHAPTER 8

Gratitude in the Workplace

Throughout *An Organizational Approach to Workplace Bullying*, recommendations for culture change, naming the behavior, training and development, communication reform, and changes in policies and procedures have been made in order to build a healthier bully-free workplace. Although the bully triad may be responsible for the mayhem, the culture of the organization often becomes the breeding ground for the toxic workplace. When organizations are looking for a quick fix to the problem, they may fire all who are responsible for the bully event. Sometimes the reaction is to promote fear in others who may be contemplating similar behaviors or misuse of power. However, firing employees may create a loss that may not be recovered concerning organizational knowledge, expertise, and brand image. In addition, firing employees for system problems may cause other highly talented employees to exit the organization.

Research has proven that any combination of interventions that include culture change, naming the behavior, training, development, communication reform, and changes in policies and procedures will yield a huge return on investment (ROI). The current chapter explores another intervention that is currently being researched, and it involves gratitude. Being appreciative and thankful are desired behaviors in organizational culture worthy of developing and have been proven to promote a high ROI concerning training during culture change. Dispositional gratitude in the workplace increases prosocial behaviors, appreciation, and coping while strengthening social relationships and fostering reciprocity.

Finding the good in the workplace bully, victim, or bystander involves gratitude and finding value in the effort that it takes to change organizational culture. Deciding to work with employees who do not get along is a significant step for an organization. It is an announcement of good faith that each employee has the capacity for change and for seeing the good in one another.

Gratitude fosters self-efficacy and is an agentic mechanism that increases the sense of personal competence and value for personally chosen goals and efforts in the workplace.[1] The level of support that team members give to one another in the workplace can be the defining factor for superior performance far above efforts derived from organizational reward and recognition alone.[2] Supportive climates build trust, better communication, and free-flowing information exchange.[2] Gratitude is a communal agent and helps employees feel connected and valued.[3] Without gratitude in the workplace, defensiveness increases, which becomes a barrier to success at every level of operation.

Sustained gratitude in the workplace helps with the maintenance of prosocial behaviors and spills over to larger groups promoting diversity consciousness.[3] Burnout is a symptom of a work environment that lacks hope and social and supervisory support.[4] Strife and conflict in the workplace and attempts to depersonalize a diverse workforce are directly related to symptoms of employee burnout.[4] An employee's master status or architectural identity is important and must be respected, honored, and supported.

Acts of gratitude help reduce the feelings of isolation created by the bully triad and is known to create high arousal states by turning shame into vitality and fear into excitement.[5] Gratitude and feelings of reciprocity of kind acts promote positive perceptions of the workplace and reduce negative biases and reflection concerning negative organizational memories.[4] During organizational change, it will be difficult to create a culture of gratitude as it is much easier to harbor a grudge because forgiveness is difficult. Forgiveness is a complex process and multidirectional, as the bully triad must work through feelings of shame and doubt. Not only must they forgive one another but bully triads must also forgive themselves.

How does an organization create an attitude of gratitude throughout the workplace when it has never really existed? Since gratitude is a positive emotion and has psychometric properties, it can be measured. If gratitude can be measured, it can also be improved and developed into an organizational trait that can be practiced and perfected.[6] Conceptualizing gratitude will help administrators look at gratitude as a system or a process toward building a culture where people get along and value one another. In the workplace, gratitude fosters reciprocity, which changes the perception of the benefactor and reduces suspicion of the motivation behind the act of kindness. Manager's find that especially true if gratitude is practiced as a normal part of everyday business.[7] Of course, everyday gratitude includes relationships between employees, upper management, and most importantly, individual reflection of gratitude for personal contribution.[5]

7Substance abuse is higher in organizations where bullying exists, and bully triads promote a vast array of unhealthy behaviors and risky lifestyle choices. In addition, it is well known that substance abuse in the workplace increases accident and injury and absentee rates.[4] According to research, gratitude is effective in the recovery of addictive behaviors.[9] For example, twelve-step alcohol and gambling treatment programs also include gratitude as part of the recovery process. Gratitude is used in these programs to promote a positive attitude and to redirect negative lamenting over areas of loss and feelings of lack of control. Loo, Tsai, Raylu, and Oei (2014) found through their research that an individual's level of gratitude is an indicator for feelings of personal competency, and when the workplace is focused on gratitude, employees focus on more positive pursuits, such as contributing at higher levels in the workplace.[9]

The research concerning gratitude in the workplace suggests several things: organizations that only focus on rewards and recognition may create unhealthy competition, but organizations that also focus on gratitude on an everyday basis may promote prosocial behavior, which may lead to a positive organizational culture. In addition, gratitude creates reciprocity, which can change how people feel about one another and how they accept the difference in the workplace. Gratitude improves coping and strengthens relationships by reducing suspicion and the need for agendas and unhealthy competition in the workplace.

Interestingly, gratitude is being used as a performance improvement tool in various industries, schools, college retention programs, recovery programs, and even prisons. Various research efforts are underway to investigate whether increasing gratitude can reduce bullying incidents on school buses, in playgrounds, and in high schools. Research has found that when gratitude does not exist in an organization, it can be manufactured or practiced until it becomes a habit or disposition. Fostering gratitude in the workplace is a low-cost/no-cost method of engaging employees on a different level that provides a great return on investment concerning training and development. Gratitude in the workplace can be measured, enhanced, and maintained through reward and recognition programs and simple things like thank-you notes.

References

1. Dhiman, S. (2010). Gifts of gratitude: Counting our blessings and appreciating the kindness of others. Business Renaissance Quarterly; Winter 2015; 5, 4: ProQuest Central.
2. LaFasto, F., & Larson, C., (2001). When teams work best. Thousand Oaks, CA: Sage Publications.
3. Grant, A., & Gino, F., (2010). A little thanks goes a long way: Explaining why gratitude expressions motivate pro-social behavior. Journal of Personality and Social Psychology Vol. 98.No. 6, 946–955.
4. Lanham, M., Rye, M., Rimsky, L., Weill, S., (2012). How gratitude relates to burnout and job satisfaction in mental health professionals. *Journal of Mental Health Counseling*, Oct 2012, 34, 4: ProQuest Central.
5. Russel, E., & Fosha, D., (2008). Transformational affects and core state in AEDP: The emergence and consolidation of joy, hope, gratitude, and confidence in (the solid goodness of) the self. Journal of Psychotherapy Integration Vol. 18, No. 2, 167–190.
6. McCullough, M., & Emmons, R., (2002).The Grateful disposition: A conceptual and empirical topography. Journal of Personality and Social Psychology Vol. 82, No. 1, 112–127.
7. Algoe, S., Haidt L., & Gable S., (2008). Beyond reciprocity: Gratitude and relationships in everyday life. Emotion Vol. 8, No. 3, 425–429.
8. Studer Group (2015). Thank you notes. Retrieved from https://www.studergroup.com/what-we-do/institutes/upcoming-institutes/taking-you-and-your-organization-to-the-next-level/taking-you-and-your-organization-to-the-next-l-%282%29/tyyo-post-event-page/temp_tools/thank-you-notes
9. Loo, J. Y., Tsai, J., Raylu, N., & Oei, T. S. (2014). Gratitude, hope, mindfulness and personal-growth initiative: Buffers or risk factors for problem gambling?. *Plos ONE, 9*(2).
10. Froh, J. J., Bono, G., & Emmons, R. (2010). Being grateful is beyond good manners: Gratitude and motivation to contribute to society among early adolescents. *Motivation And Emotion, 34*(2), 144-157.

Gratitude Assessment Rubric

Name _____ Date _____

Optimal Criteria	1	2	3	Rating
I am grateful throughout each day.	I am grateful on occasion.	If I place gratitude on my to-do list, I am grateful often.	I find new opportunities to feel grateful every day.	
I am able to capture moments of gratitude during stress-filled days.	I cannot feel gratitude when I am stressed.	If I calm down enough, I can remember to be grateful.	I can find moments of gratitude even during stress-filled moments.	
I discover new ways to look at those things that I may have taken for granted.	I am unaware of the things that I take for granted.	It is enough to be grateful once for an ongoing gift or blessing.	I take random surveys of the good things and the lessons learned in my life and remember to be grateful.	
I can shift my focus from feeling entitled to becoming humble and grateful.	I feel that I have worked hard and deserve the good in my life.	I have worked hard, and I remember to be grateful for the important moments or success in my life.	I have worked hard and reflect often that without the help of others and my higher power, my growth and success would not be a reality.	
I can be filled with gratitude during sadness, conflict, and illness.	I find it very difficult to feel grateful when I experience challenges.	At the first sign of improvement when I am involved in a difficult situation, I feel grateful.	I am able to see a difficult situation through to its resolution and continue to be filled with gratitude.	

Total _____

CHAPTER 9

Managing the Gifted and the Ungifted

Creating sameness in an organization where every system has been cleansed of discrepancies and redesigned to promote a healthier bully-free environment is optimal except for one or two things. A homogenous work environment may not arouse innovation and creativity, and sameness may lead to less flexibility and appreciation for the gifted employee and the employee with learning or attention deficit disorders. It is the gray areas in the organizational structure that allow for exceptions and exceptional staff to flourish and thrive. It is the ambiguous areas of the workplace where mission statements and employee loyalty and commitment are tested.

Managers in the workforce often do not realize that those pesky childhood labels such as attention deficit / hyperactivity disorder, Asperger's syndrome, learning disorders, conduct disorders, and anxiety do not just disappear upon adulthood. Remnants of the disorders are manifested in behaviors that are often labeled as poor time management, low productivity, lack of attention to detail, being accident-prone, and social loafing. Therefore, behavioral disorders are not factors to be considered concerning accommodation and access in the workplace but, instead, are often penalized during performance reviews. Also, reward and recognition programs are just out of reach of the employees with the above issues because these programs are based on the elite employee.

Additionally, gifted children and all their complexities grow up to be employees who do not know how to conform or share their innovation and creativity appropriately. Power struggles or bullying often develop in the workplace because of these complex social disorders, and some members eventually become marginalized because of their gifts and their cognitive and social dis-ease struggle. According to research, gifted people have trouble with social appropriateness almost to the level of displaying social disability in the workplace.[1] Common behaviors are conflicts with authority, high sensitivity, lack of perseverance and discipline, and demanding, irreverent natures.

Highly intelligent people are often seen as know-it-alls with a negative perception of the world, which makes teams and administrators less likely to seek as much knowledge as they should from these individuals.[1] In addition, a gifted person's inappropriate behaviors coupled with the avoidance behaviors of peers can lead to isolation and withdrawal from their gifts and normal levels of creativity and productivity.[2]

Sameness in job description and policy will not encourage gifted employees to adapt and participate fully and fairly in the work environment. In addition, not only do degrees in giftedness need to be identified but reward and recognition should also be based on growth with future opportuntities.[1] While there are areas where some behaviors cannot be tolerated, creating a learning environment or learning society will help satisfy some of the emotional and intellectual cravings of the gifted individual and will stimulate other employees to be innovative because the workplace will become a learning dynamic and not just a static pool of policies.

Employees with ADD and ADHD struggle with self-regulation and are easily distracted from their assigned tasks and responsibilities.[4] Employees with attention deficits have trouble with time management and tend to lose track of goals.[4] Of course, employees with attention deficit disorders do not mean that they cannot contribute and become valuable employees. Still, it does mean that their managers need to understand their attention issues and provide a work environment that complements or balances these behavioral challenges. For example, offering reward and recognition based on smaller increments of achievement can be very motivating for these employees.[4] Managers that provide both tangible and intangible rewards for positive behavior and time management are more successful with ADD or ADHD employees because they recognize their employee's strengths and weaknesses.[4]

Unless intelligence or learning disabilities are revealed at the time of application, a manager may not realize that he or she is dealing with an employee with special needs. Sometimes, through voluntary testing, an employee may discover his or her IQ or EQ and, in a trusting environment, might share testing information with their closest supervisor.[2] In a situation where termination is imminent for an employee with social problems, it might be necessary for the EAP to make the necessary arrangements or suggestions for testing. Information from IQ and EQ testing can provide information that may identify accommodation needs as well as direction for behavioral management programs and self-development programs. Managers and supervisors must be interested enough in their employee's success to understand the level of autonomy, trust, and motivation needed for those employees with social dis-ease to participate fully. Providing safe environments and work that is both challenging and suited for their gifts or accommodation needs will help employees achieve their best success.[3]

When organizations opt for culture change as a way to deter bully triads, it is important to recognize that sameness and rigid compliance of countless policies may subdue creativity and innovation. The same flexibility that allowed the bully triad to develop is the same flexibility that is needed to foster creativity and innovation across gifts and disabilities. When giftedness and learning or attention deficit disorders are recognized, it is essential to seek accommodation and to reevaluate reward and recognition programs. In addition, it is essential to continue to reduce ambiguity in organizational policies to support the marginalized and to reduce predatory behaviors of the bully.

Adams's equity theory concerning job motivation states that employees try to balance a list of very subjective conditions concerning inputs and outputs.[5] Each individual employee can list what he or she puts into the job and what return is expected concerning both tangible and intangible rewards. Employees become demotivated whenever they feel that their inputs are not being fairly rewarded by outputs, which, of course, is based on their personal subjective rating scale.[5] Aligning reward and recognition with an organizational measurement and rating system for inputs and outputs may be very challenging in a diverse workplace, especially with a talent pool that consists of bullies, gifted employees, and the marginalized. During organizational culture change to a bully-free workplace, it is beneficial to review policies and procedures, performance review systems, employee perception of inputs and outputs, and reward and recognition programs for congruency and to clearly communicate the aggregate and agreed-upon expectations.

However, bully triads that exist prior to organizational culture change thrive on the ambiguous areas where barriers are indistinct and confusing. It is ambiguity that provides the leverage that bullies need for many different control points. For example, bullies have tremendous political stamina, and they can sway even the most experienced manager to release a positive review. After all, ambiguity is the fuel that kick-starts unfair competition and positioning in the workplace. It is also the leverage that bullies use to overpower the gifted, learning or attention deficit employee, or employees with invisible disabilities.

Managing gifted employees and marginalized employees requires acceptance and empathy. It also requires knowing your employees enough to be able to identify their struggles and to put in place accommodation and support measures, as well as boundaries, as needed. Should managers create a state of advocacy for all conflict involving performance outliers? Only if they value critical thinking more than they do persuasion and lobbying for justice.[6] Moving from a culture of advocacy to one of inquiry produces collaborative results that tend to support organizational objectives.[7] According to Greenleaf (2002), anyone can lead perfect people, but to lead imperfect people requires acceptance and empathy. Creating a council of equals involves a willingness to be the leader of the process by promoting critical thought and by giving the tools for change to the employees.

References

1. Corten, F., Nauta, N., Ronner, S., (2006). Highly gifted employees – Key to innovation? International HRD Conference. Amsterdam, Holland.

2. Noks Nauta and Frans Corten (Kumar Jamdagni, trans.) Gifted adults at work. Tijdschrift voor Bedrijfs- en Verzekeringsgeneeskunde (Journal for Occupational and Insurance Physicians). 2002 10(11) 332-335.Retrieved from http://sengifted.org/archives/articles/gifted-adults-in-work

3. Nauta, A., (2011). Recognize your gifted employees, give them work that suits them, autonomy and trust and talk about their needs and motivation. Retrieved from http://www.12manage.com/myview.asp?KN=2561.

4. Lipman, V., (2012). How to manage employees with ADD/ADHD. http://www.forbes.com/sites/victorlipman/2012/10/02/how-to-manage-employees-with-addadhd/

5. Baack, D., Reilly, M., & Minnick, C., & (2014). *The five function of effective management* (2nd ed.). San Diego, CA: Bridgepoint Education, Inc.

6. Greenleaf, R., (2002). *Servant leadership.* Mahwah, NJ: Paulist Press.

7. Maccoby. M., (2008). Why people follow the leader in *Harvard Business Review on the persuasive leader.* Boston, Mass: Harvard Business School Publishing Corporation.

CHAPTER 10

---◆---

Bully Triad Behaviors That Defeat Organizational Wellness

According to Witte (2010), "Man is a pack animal; hardwired to belong to a herd, relying on numbers to allow protection during growth, exponentiation of learning and for procreation and sustainability of the species." Health and well-being are dependent on the level and quality of socialization (Witte, 2010). When organizational culture fails to focus on socialization as a necessity of life, dysfunctional relationships develop, and often, bully triads across divisions begin to surface. Witte states that behavior is modified when you need to socialize; we have to socialize to belong and to acquire tacit commitments from others to agree to a form of mutuality that is essential for all forms of survival (2010).

The current chapter is a meta-analysis or sampling of bully triad behaviors or unresolved managerial issues that may threaten organizational wellness. The degree of harm will depend on how the organization names the behavior, the toxicity of the organization, and the culture of the organization. Every issue listed is grouped according to the wellness categories outlined in the Vital Life Community program, which was created by Bill Witte. These categories address the full spectrum of wellness, which are the social, spiritual, physical, occupational, environmental, nutritional, emotional, and intellectual dimensions of wellness. A balanced life that addresses the entire spectrum of wellness will promote *fun and function* versus *frailty and failure* (Witte, 2010). The "*fun and function* versus *frailty and failure*" philosophy applies to organizations too, which are nothing more than a collective with the same basic wellness needs to function. If bully triad behaviors are identified as issues or a threat to organizational wellness, then problems such as the ones listed below can be resolved with training and focus on the mission and values of the organization. It is when nothing is done and advocacy is absent that even with the smallest infraction, it will seem like a personal assault.

Sampling of Bully Triad Behaviors

Behaviors/Cultures That Reduce Physical Wellness in the Workplace		
Dismissive gestures	Positioning	Pushing
Resource hoarding	Destruction of property	Barricading
Stealing	Harming	Disregard for safety
Invasion of space	Creation of hazards	Promoting injury or falls
Assault	Physical harassment	Vandalizing
Poor turn-taking	Intimidation	Confrontational communication
Refusal to assist	Unwanted contact	Arranging barriers
Disorganization	Slowing production on purpose	Increasing the pace of work inappropriately
Creating unnecessary downtime	Improperly maintaining equipment or tools, making work harder	Failure to report safety issues
Unfair work schedules and employee allocation	Distributing unfair workloads	Showing favoritism concerning work spaces and supplies
Refusal to provide accommodation	Setting unrealistic goals and deadlines	Assignment of substandard material to work with
Failure to provide the basic needs of the job	Creating understaffed conditions	Refusal to clean up spills and hazards
Failure to provide personal protection equipment	Failure to upgrade work stations	Interruptions to training and mastery
Failure to inform the next shift about current issues	Failure to provide ergonomic work stations	Excessive monitoring

Behaviors/Cultures That Reduce Emotional Wellness in the Workplace		
Intimidation	Teasing	Mocking others
Belittling because of position in organization or socioeconomic standing	Put-downs that are directed at a person's identity, race, and culture	Excluding others from teams and groups
Public or private humiliation	Blaming others without proper fact finding	Embarrassing others in meetings
Spreading rumors	Spreading lies	Tormenting others
Insulting	Threatening	Debasing the reputation of others
Taking away personal rights	Restricting creative expression	Pressured to act against values
Pressured to act unethically	Forced isolation from social groups at work	Threats to abandon friendship
Disrespectful of the ideas and opinions of others	Derogatory and slanderous statements toward others	Frightening others or insensitive play
Minimizing reports of verbal/physical abuse	Questioning someone's worth or value	Highlighting the insecurities of others
Restricting the voice of others	Discounting the opinions and ideas of others	Explosive accusations
Faultfinding with everyday processes	Expressions of disgust directed toward others	Distorted propaganda about the stability of the organization
Arrogant justification of bad behavior	Focus on the powerlessness of subordinates	Making threats to job security

Behaviors/Culture That Reduce Intellectual Wellness in the Workplace		
Plagiarism	Hoarding knowledge	Insufficient training
Disrespect of the mission and vision	Exclusion from decision-making	Total disregard for learning styles
Providing false positive reviews	Unexplained or justified censorship	Disorganization of projects
Impossible budget restrictions	Encountering barriers to data needed to finish projects	Refusing to meet the technology needs of employees
Not factoring time for research and review	Dismissing personalities and leadership styles	Working without feedback
Refusing to accommodate learning deficits	Management dismissal of newly acquired degrees or certifications	Refusing to accommodate vision and hearing loss
Correcting employees publicly	Humiliating employees for mispronouncing words because of hearing deficits	Vague reporting channels
Changing ownership of intellectual work	Collecting group support to devalue a project	Comparing or devaluing educational gains/ success
Forming intellectual work groups based on socioeconomic status	Performance improvement reviews that are biased	Ego-driven role theft
Lack of delegated authority	Poorly defined project success/completion	Unawareness of project termination plans
Ignoring language barriers	Entrenched incompetence	Unbridled brilliance and unreasonable productivity work bursts

Behaviors/Culture That Reduce Social Wellness in the Workplace		
Being self-interested	Cliques	Narcissistic teams
Creating socioeconomic boundaries	"Survival of the fitness" mentality	Hazing of new members
Insufficient orientation	Fostering a culture of silo mentalities	Exclusive celebrations, parties, and luncheons
Alienating employees from their natural ability to connect	Marginalizing already oppressed groups	Inability to socialize because of lack of funds for lunch, dinners, or trips
Inappropriate relationships	"Everyone does it" mentality, even though there are policies to prevent the behavior	Social loafing within projects or teams
Sharing too much personal information	Lack of interpreters for language and culture	Inappropriate use of social media
Disrespect for introverts or shyness	Addressing hygiene issues	Ignoring dress codes
Lack of honesty	Selective confidentiality	Sacrificing coworkers for selfish reasons
Acts of retaliation	Lack of group integrity	Identity theft
Inequities in pay and benefits	Ineffective damage control	Poor attitudes
Addiction and substance abuse issues at work	Frightening coworkers with practical jokes	Double-talk
Insincere apologies	Proximity issues that place privacy at risk	Reducing work hours based on favoritism

Behaviors/Culture That Reduce Spiritual Wellness in the Workplace		
Negativity	Burnout	Unresolved ethical dilemmas
Pressure to steal from or cheat the organization	Pressure to compromise personal beliefs	Refusal to recognize autonomy
Ridiculing religious practices	Posting vulgarity	Offensive speech
Tempting the religious beliefs of others	Feeling that gifts and talents are not needed or wanted	Feelings and opinions are rarely validated
Dismissing humility as weakness	Demoralizing employees	Stifling employee potential
Fear of disclosure	Distrust	Failure to forgive
Religious discrimination and failure to accommodate	Interreligious misunderstandings	Heightened sense of religious bias for promotions and opportunities
Disrespect for lack of religious affiliation	Lack of flexible hours to accommodate religious holidays	Unfair religious holiday swapping
Policies that conflict with religious attire	Questioning the sincerity of another's faith	Theology debates that exceed comfort levels of the group
Lack of meditation or quiet break areas	Failure to provide privacy for prayer breaks	Evangelizing without consent
Questioning a person's purpose	Lack of grief support for loss of coworkers	Lack of understanding of how crises are processed in different cultures
Questioning the validity of affiliation or faith	Lack of reintegration support for demotions	Conflicts based on transference of roles and position

Behaviors/Culture That Reduce Nutritional Wellness in the Workplace		
Sabotaging diets	Unlabeled allergens	Scheduling meetings during lunch or breaks
Reducing break and lunchtimes	Failure to remove used or outdated foods from pantry or refrigerators	Disrespect of food-related cultural celebrations
Disrespect of ethnic food selections	Food-related events that ignore diet restrictions	Limiting healthier vending selections
Food-related events that ignore cultural beliefs	Strong offensive odors or scents	Food allergy harassment
Separation of food areas from work areas	Humiliating employees with eating disorders	Questioning the seriousness of digestive illnesses
Ridiculing thinness or obesity	Lack of cleanliness in break areas	Pointing out misaligned teeth or chewing problems
Promoting food/diet fads at work	Sharing or pushing diet pills and concoctions	Leaving food in refrigerators or out in common areas to spoil
Eating food that belongs to other employees	Limited food access	Lunch breaks that are not free of work duties
Lack of private areas to pray or meditate before/after meals	Refusal to accommodate mini meals or snacks for medical purposes	Hostile dining area with pranks or inappropriate behavior
Storytelling that suppresses appetite	Workload pressure that burdens employees to shorten lunch breaks	Failure to inform others of free food or vendor gifts
Deducting pay for missed lunch breaks	Forced lunch gatherings and lack of concern for social anxiety	Close contact during meals with hostile workers

Behaviors/Culture That Reduce Occupational Wellness in the Workplace		
Creating barriers to cross-functional solutions	Refusal to share common goals	Corruption of teams or groups
Lack of ownership	Refusal to accept change	Lack of engagement of peers
Starting rumors about job insecurity	Lack of synergy between groups or teams	Priority confusion, or "everything is a crisis"
Ignoring the organizational chart	Refusal to work with divisions and corporations	Going over someone's head for personal gain
Harboring resources	Poor turn-taking	Evidence collecting for only one side of the conflict
No career development	Pay inequities	Stressful pay structures
Failure to inspire confidence in the organization	Letting important credentials and certifications expire	No investigation for complaints, boss avoids conflict
Conducting personal business at work	Unfulfilling, meaningless work	Coworkers in it for the money only
Workers who are always in the act of exiting	Workaholics who expect the same from everyone else	Unable to leverage strengths in the workplace
Expected to take work home and continue working	Pay below industry standards	Nobody respects the chain of command
Poor management styles that go unchecked	Unproductive meetings	Rewarding seniority and not merit
Vacations are suspended or nonexistent	Raises and reviews are skipped for long periods	No one ever gets fired, and incompetence is rewarded
Strict IT rules that inhibit productivity	Being treated as an interchangeable part	No face-to-face time with the boss

Behaviors/Culture That Reduce Environmental Wellness in the Workplace		
Nervous workplace	Irritated coworkers	Persistent conflict
Creating unsafe conditions by refusing accommodation	Poor distribution of safety equipment	Failure to assign proper credit of work
Showdowns at work	Lack of mentorship	Using coworkers for personal gain
Micromanagement	Discrimination and bias	Managerial unresponsiveness to questions and concerns
Road rage	Littering	Assigning mind-numbing work
Tardy coworkers	Coworkers with bad habits/manners	Distracted coworkers
Long vacancies and unfilled job positions	Failure to report abuse of coworkers	Rewarding seniority and not merit
Off-duty worry about work	Poor support for expats and their families	Too many bosses
Unmanned work stations	Psychologically terrorizing others with hidden disabilities	Employees who threaten litigation rather than compromise
Entrapment	Underemployed	Poor retention
Privacy leaks and lack of confidentiality	Watercooler gossip	Weak hiring and screening practices
Poor policies and follow-ups concerning bullying	Not confronting rule breakers	Policies that do not apply to everyone

In a toxic culture, many of the behaviors listed above are directed toward other employees who take the abuse in silence. It becomes very risky for an employee to complain of ill-treatment in a workplace where these behaviors are not identified as antisocial or bully-like. However, in a healthy organizational culture, an employee will speak up when injustice occurs because there is a platform already established with anchors and advocates ready to clarify expectations.

CHAPTER 11

Just a Few Stories of Bullying

The current chapter is devoted to a few stories of bullying. Many more stories were told as members of various organizations were interviewed during the research phase of *An Organizational Approach to Workplace Bullying*; however, these stories will not be shared in the current book because many individuals still felt fearful about the events and their unresolved anger. However, the stories that were shared are anonymous to protect the identity of the employee; otherwise, the wording and content remain as the submitted versions. When reading the stories carefully and while taking the time to interpret the losses experienced by the organization and the hurt expressed by the employee, it is easy to start adding up the cost of lost trust, dedication, organizational knowledge, and brand image.

***

I had a supervisor once who did not really understand what we were trying to accomplish. He had a temper and would fly off the handle at minor things. He would hit things like a wall or a door. He stopped doing that at work, but one day he came in to work with a cast on his hand.

***

I got my first full-time teaching job right out of college. I was young and optimistic, with idealistic dreams about making the world a better place by inspiring our future leaders! Initially, when I began teaching, I got along well with all the staff and students. All the teachers were very nice to me, and I felt honored to be teaching at such a prestigious school. Other teachers dreamed of working here—there were so many opportunities and resources that just weren't available at smaller school districts. It was a dream come true and such an achievement for my very first teaching job!

The organization was a school district that had started small and had grown considerably in a short period of time to become one of the largest districts in the area. Because of the growth, there were the "old school" people who had grown up in that town and the "new people" who had only recently moved to the area. There was often income and education disparity noticeable between the two groups. It didn't take me long to realize that there was also a definite hierarchy in place among the teachers, as is common in many workplace environments. "The good ole boy's club," as it was so often referred to, seemed to be the group of individuals who had been in the town the most number of generations and had the most pull when it came to making decisions. If someone higher up made a decision that wasn't popular within the group, they found ways to change the outcome.

For the first few years, I was successfully able to stay out of most of the politics that took place at the school. I went to work, taught my classes, and really took pride in upholding the responsibility that my job entailed. I began to look for ways to offer more options to my students so that a wider base of students could be reached in a variety of nontraditional ways. As more of my efforts were being noticed by the administration, there were more and more grumblings from the teachers within my department. I was one of three females in a male-dominated department and the only new person in our entire group who hadn't grown up in the town. The rest of the department had families who had been in the area for years and had participated in the same activities together, forming strong bonds. I was the newcomer who was shaking up the way things had been done for decades.

I was asked by the administration to create new curriculums and classes as well as to review the current class offerings. As the enrollment of the school continued to increase, our department had to hire new teachers to keep up with the growing numbers, as well as offer new classes to accommodate all the students. When the change happened, our location in the school spread out, and our department became less centralized. The department head who had always held our group together retired, and with the addition of some new dominant personalities and the loss of my only friend and supporter in the department, the entire atmosphere of our department and work environment shifted. I became the outcast who was making the rest of the team look bad. I was mocked, criticized, and ostracized for my efforts to reach the students in innovative ways that would require much more effort on the part of the teacher. The department was used to doing things a certain way and had no intention of changing to make more work for themselves in order to better serve the changing needs of the students. It seemed I was a little too eager to go the extra mile, and because of that, I became the target of their bullying. It appeared to be a game to see how far they could push me before I would quit or self-destruct.

There are many examples of the types of childish behavior the adults I worked with would resort to in an attempt to restore their superiority over a peer, but one situation that exemplifies the ruthlessness of the individuals in my department relates to an additional job I was offered within the department. At the current point in time, I had been completely cut off from my other coworkers, had lost my office to a newer teacher, shared a classroom with the new teacher (who I only saw when she wanted to complain about something I did she didn't like), and never saw another adult during the teaching day unless I made a point to go visit a different wing of the school. I felt as if I had no support, had no space of my own to feel settled and work, and felt like I was always in a toxic environment when I was around my department. I dreaded coming to work if I knew I would have to face one of my department members that day. The students were the only reason I would get out of bed to come in to work most days. Sadly, they would often mention to me how poorly the other teachers in my department treated me and talked about me in front of them. They would ask me why the teachers didn't like me. It was a shame the students had to see adults behaving so poorly.

Interestingly, an outside organization was interested in hiring a person from within the school for a part-time after-school job. I had been approached as the perfect person to fill the role. I was very excited for the opportunity and had all the necessary qualifications and certifications that would make me the ideal candidate for the position. I had two interviews to fully understand what would be expected of me, who I would be overseeing, and other details of the new job. It was an opportunity I had been considering for some time as it would use more fully the continuing education I had received upon completing my master's degree outside of education. The organization was excited about having me on board, and I was thrilled about the possibilities to change some of the dynamics of my current job that were less than desirable. It would provide an outlet for me that I didn't have in my teaching (which I still very much enjoyed despite the hostile environment) to collaborate with positive and supportive staff.

The night before I was planning to accept the job offer, I received a phone call from a friend of mine. She had been doing her student teaching at the school where I worked within my department, but I never saw her during the day. She told me that she overheard some of the teachers in the department talking between classes about my new job offer. No one was happy with it. No one wanted me to take the job. At lunch that day, all the teachers in the department got together and discussed ways they would sabotage me if I were to accept the job. With the new job, I would be overseeing most of them in their after-school roles *and* filling a role that had traditionally always been filled by a male. There were some pretty harsh words said about my abilities as a female (even though I had more training in that area than all of them combined) and very specific examples of how they would make sure that I failed at that job if I were to accept it.

The responses were all very shocking to me. I was very grateful for the chance to know the information before making my final decision, although I had suspected they would not be happy about the news. It proved to be quite a dilemma for me. I knew I was qualified, and I had every confidence that I could do the job well in addition to withstanding the efforts to undermine my authority in the position. Part of me wanted to take the job just to show them I was tough and could take it! The other part of me knew that my life was already stressful enough with all the bullying I had to deal with on a daily basis from my department. Did I really need to add more stress to my life just to prove a point? I had already looked for new jobs outside the school district. Only one school in the area was hiring in my subject area, and there was absolutely no ability for creative curriculum and diversity in the student body. Unfortunately for my mental health, if I wanted to feel like I was contributing in a positive way to the growth of the students, I would have to stay at the district.

It was with a heavy heart that I told the organization the next day that I was declining the job, much to their dismay. I was honest about my reasons, and because they had some understanding about how the politics worked at the school, they did understand. They told me if I ever changed my mind, the door was open to explore other opportunities. Interestingly, the person who ended up taking the job was also a woman. However, she was the daughter of one of the good ole boys club members. So that must have made her an acceptable candidate to my department, and she was never harassed.

***

After a meeting, a fellow director smugly told me that I had mispronounced a word in the meeting. I told her that I was hearing impaired and that I would probably mispronounce words from time to time. So I asked her how the correct pronunciation sounded, and she bared her teeth and very hatefully spoke the word that I had mispronounced. The word was *labyrinth*, and I think she ruined all my future thoughts about walking in a labyrinth to meditate.

***

I had corrected some processes that were making the microorganism count high at a beverage plant, and the sanitation crews were not happy. They retaliated in little ways, like hiding test kits and locking a swinging door from the lab to production, which resulted in damage to my hand as I was moving at production speed to test a product and collided with the locked door. I left the organization soon after.

***

Production supervisor was a hothead, and any time the line went down, he would begin to throw things and cuss. It was quite frightening, and although most employees were not fearful for themselves or their job security, they did feel fearful that the supervisor would harm himself.

***

The only bullying that I received at that time while working at a large data center in 1972–75 was because I was a woman. We were relegated to the jobs of secretary or menial accountant. When I was promoted from executive secretary to the director of personnel to the first-ever customer service supervisor, I became the first woman supervisor at the organization. At the time, my boss was in the same building. Within two months, the organization did an across-the-board cut of every manager on my boss's level. Thus, his boss, who was stationed in New York City, became my boss. It was cool because he gave me the ability to make up the procedures that I needed, to hire a staff on my own, and basically run things like I wanted to. I just had to send a weekly report to him about what I had done, how many system failures, how many users, and any unusual problems. I spoke to all the lawyers and accountants across the United States and England by phone when they had difficulty formulating a search to retrieve the documents they desired or when the system would crash. I had two five-line phones on my desk that would light up like a Christmas tree when the system would crash! I had a spacious second-floor corner office with an entire wall of glass windows. The transplanted New Yorker who directed our fledgling business as president came into my office at least five or six times a day to "read" the computer equipment in my office, which was the heartbeat of our company. He also would be in my office when the system would crash (which was often in those days) to see how quickly the problem could be repaired because the organizational personnel across the street at the main office would communicate with me. I really felt like I had achieved the perfect job.

Now I suppose you are thinking that the bullying I received was from the high-level executives running our business. But you would be wrong. The treasurer, personnel director, accountant, vice president, and president, who were all men, treated me with respect. They did not see me as the executive secretary who was promoted to customer service supervisor. They saw me as the customer service supervisor. I was flown to New York City to meet the big boss and be included in strategy meetings for the future of the organization. The bullying was from the older secretarial worker whose desk was right outside my office. Because her boss's office was on the other side of the hallway, there was no other place to put her besides directly outside my office door. Thus, she could hear every conversation I had every day as I always left my door open. Even in my executive secretarial job, she and I had never been on the same level because she was a secretary from the office pool. In hindsight, I guess she was envious of my promotion. She made my life miserable. Every time I left my office to go to the president's office, she made a hateful comment. And there was also one when I returned to my office. I was not about to let her ruin my dream job, so I just ignored her. I did not take my problem to the personnel director, because in those days, you just handled problems on your own. The personnel director did the hiring, firing, and promoting. He did not handle petty problems. Her behaviors went on for weeks, months, and years. After a while, I just worked with my door closed as I could hear her toxic conversations about me with other like-minded steno pool individuals as they talked at her desk. It worked better with my door closed, but I still had to put up with the hateful comments when we would be in the restroom or lunchroom at the same time.

My husband and I had decided that we were not going to have any children when we married. We dated for seven years and had been married for four years. We had built a beautiful home a few years earlier and were furnishing it with the money both of us made at our jobs. I started giving serious thought to the fact that perhaps the workplace in the story was not what I wanted to do for the rest of my life, as the lady was causing a considerable amount of stress in my life. As strange as it sounds now, being a woman in a position of authority was very unique and practically unheard of in the early 1970s. After an unusually hurtful exchange when returning to my office, I sat at my desk and cried. I guess she had finally broken my spirit. I will never forget calling my husband and telling him that I wanted to start a family. There was complete silence on the other end of the line. He finally said that we would discuss it at home that evening, which we did. We discussed the obvious pros and the cons, which included not being able to continue our current lifestyle or finish furnishing our home. We were in total agreement that we would start a family. It took us one-and-one-half years before we conceived our daughter, during which time I continued my job. I was five months pregnant before anyone suspected anything at work because pantsuits with jackets helped me keep our secret. I took maternity leave and never went back. Of course, we were thrilled to be parents and were fortunate enough to have a second daughter.

We had agreed to live on my husband's salary and that I would be a stay-at-home mother. We never looked back and have enjoyed our family tremendously.

Who knows how long I would have worked if it had not been for the lady right outside my office door being so vitriolic. Fortunately, office procedures have changed for the better. Now, behavior such as that would never have been tolerated. Human resource departments have a much longer reach into the day-to-day dealings within an office today. Women in positions of power are common throughout the world. But in the early 1970s, things were a lot different.

***

I was a young waitress, and tips were few most days in the '70s. I remember a non-English speaking mother and her two children who had walked from the airport to the restaurant when their ride did not show. They must have walked five miles and were hungry and tired. They refused to order from the menu and only wanted water to drink. I gave them my tips for the day, which amounted to $1.70, and ordered for them. After they left, I was threatened by my supervisor that he would fire me if he ever caught me helping nonpaying customers again. I told him that I paid for their meal, and he still threatened to fire me. I was a single mother who depended on a meager waitressing job to support my family.

***

I have been a victim of bullying in the workplace. It began when a new manager was assigned to the group. The new manager and the senior system administrator that was hired shortly before that quickly struck up what appeared to be a friendship. Within weeks the new manager (Art) and the senior system administrator (Tom) were having hushed conversations in Tom's cube, within earshot of my cube. Additionally, I began to get corrected on my behavior and performance in the office during my one-on-one biweekly meetings with the new manager. There were even instances where Art would call Tom in to participate in my one-on-one. Every complaint they had was unsubstantiated, but it quickly became apparent that the primary person complaining was Tom. Tom continued to get more responsibilities, and I was given many more menial tasks. None of my accomplishments were being recognized, and my first yearly performance review had slipped two points on a five-point scale. When I attempted to bring the issue up to the director over our group, it was met with deaf ears. I was left with no alternatives except to bring it directly to HR or to simply put up with it until the manager was replaced. Eventually that manager was put in a "lead" role after a reorganization, thus not being a manager anymore, and had subsequently been laid off.

***

Because of a personal conflict, Jane and Sam were having issues in their workplace. Neither was speaking to the other, but Sam had decided she would prevent Jane from receiving mail and phone messages. Where before Sam had given messages to Jane immediately, now she walked into the employee workroom and placed her messages there. The conflict made Jane's job, which was fast-paced and unpredictable, difficult. Jane had to walk past Sam's desk to get the messages, and each time, Sam made sure she was whispering and laughing with a colleague. When the issue of messages came up with Jane's supervisor, a meeting was called with Sam, Jane, and their mutual supervisor. Sam was very angry and wanted to discuss the personal issue. Their supervisor allowed the situation to continue, even to the point where Sam was yelling at Jane loud enough to be heard outside the conference room for almost ten minutes. Several workers heard clearly Sam's perception of the personal issue and couldn't help listening from their workstations.

***

I requested that an elderly patient be brought to a place to view his favorite activity programming, which required the aide to get the resident presentable to transport to a public area of the facility. The aide was so angry she dry-shaved the resident, creating pain and irritation for the nonverbal patient. As a bully, the person was indestructible and covered her tracks. After, I made sure that I only asked for the patient to be up on her off days. I shudder when I remember the story and the terrible incident.

CHAPTER 12

Lasting Unquestionable Forgiveness

There have been several times in my life when I thought that I had forgiven bully events that were directed toward me personally. But I found that when meeting the bully again, my original anger was rekindled. Somehow, in my ignorance or innocence, I believed that life would change the bully and that remorse or growth would be apparent. For example, I remember, as a middle school student, I was riding home on the school bus when a couple of high school boys decided to pick on me just for their fun and amusement. The two boys had just finished a science experiment at school and were taking their six-volt batteries home when they got the bright idea to shock me in the back of the head with their live-wired batteries while making war whoops to mock my Indian heritage. Unfortunately, the abuse lasted the entire bus trip home because I was in an assigned seat and was not allowed to move and the bus driver ignored my call for help and attempts to dodge the attacks.

Many years later, while working at a community college, I ran into the lead bully, who was also a teacher, only to have him turn to sneer at me and then dismiss my presence. My forgiveness was challenged that day as I could not believe that his perspective had not changed through time or education. I felt sorry for him and his students. I was angered all over again, enough that it made me question my faith and my ability to forgive.

Since then, several bully events at work have challenged my faith in myself concerning forgiveness and returning to business as usual. When you are bullied without intervention or an advocate, it changes how you respond professionally. For me, I was always on the defensive, or I found myself aggressively trying to prove the wrongness of the bully's actions. For example, I had finally completed my master's degree, and I changed my email signature to show the new designation. But I was admonished by another director, who stated that I should not add my new credentials because other employees had worked just as hard for their education as I did even though they might not have the degrees to show for it. I certainly had not added my credentials to be viewed as better than anyone; however, part of my job involved working with the public and higher education, and adding my new credentials would have fostered the additional networks that I needed to do my job. I removed my designations to maintain the peace, but when the bully had completed her degrees and posted her new designations in her signature, I knew I had been duped.

The story above was not a large-scale bully event, but it was followed by many other annoying attempts to place me in a subservient position. I found myself questioning my ability to forgive again because I was reaching my breaking point. The culture and environment supported the bully in the story, who not only bullied me but also many others. A lifetime of experience with bully types is what led to the research and writing of *An Organizational Approach to Workplace Bullying.* I wanted to understand the bully triad so that every time a new bully event occurred, I would respond professionally and with compassion and a lasting unquestionable forgiveness.

The research for *An Organizational Approach to Workplace Bullying* involved conducting a meta-analysis of methods to improve organizational culture, as listed in previous chapters, and it involved personal reflection and connecting to my higher power. Pastor Dan Hicks stated that "the bullies of the world have limited understanding in social skills; and therefore, lack the ability to live peaceably with others. They tend to be selfish and demanding to get what they want, rather than think of the needs of others" (Hicks, 2015). In addition, "The Bible teaches us in Galatians 5:22—But the fruit of the Spirit is love, joy, peace, longsuffering, gentleness, goodness, and faith" (Hicks, 2015).

The bully triad receives the full attention of the administrator or CEO when the organizational brand image is damaged or there is a loss or decline in retention of brand knowledge, productivity, employee satisfaction, and customer satisfaction. In addition, when ethical decision-making is compromised or the values and mission of the organization are not revered anymore, administrators and CEOs take note and begin to assign a dollar value on the damage. But before the bully triad reached a point of no return, a war of discrepancies concerning gaps in incongruent policies, values and beliefs, biased performance appraisals, uneven distribution of power and resources, and poorly defined inappropriate behaviors and relationships was nurtured by the organization.

An Organizational Approach to Workplace Bullying is a book that offers various assessment methods to change organizational culture and to begin the healing process. Examining unmet needs and promoting the removal of certain unhealthy norms that may exist will help reduce the longevity of future workplace bullies and ease the distress of victims and bystanders. More importantly, change will bring about forgiveness so that the very same employees who battled against one another or who were fearful of one another may find the peace to work under one organizational mission again.

ABOUT THE AUTHOR

Debra is an adjunct Instructor at Sinclair Community College and serves as an associate faculty member at the University of Arizona Global Campus and Forbes School of Business and Technology. She is an advisory board member for the Mental Health Technology Program at Sinclair Community College and is a certified Vital Life Community Consultant through THW Design. She also serves as an online academic distance learning specialist for Hondros School of Nursing. Debra is a pre-approved instructor of the NCCAP program for activity directors.

Dr. Stewart earned an Associate's of Fine Arts Degree from Sinclair Community College and a Bachelor of Science Degree from Charter Oak State, graduating with honors. She received a Master's in Business Administration and a Master's in Teaching & Learning with Technology from Ashford University with honors. Debra has also completed a Psy.D. in Organizational Psychology specializing in health and wellness from the University of the Rockies.

Dr. Stewart working with Dr. Andree Swanson of the Forbes School of Business and Technology, recently won the Forbes School of Business and Technology University Fellowship Program Grant to research the topic of preferred learning styles of persons living with dementia and unit productivity.

Debra has worked in long-term care for over 30 years. She has many awards and presentations to her credit, including being nominated for the Ohio Assisted Living Association Outstanding Activity Director award in 2007 and recognized with the Ohio Health Care Association Professional Achievement Award in 2009. She was also awarded The Great Award by the Association of Private Sector Colleges and Universities in 2012.

Dr. Stewart is passionate about improving the quality of life for senior adult care and job satisfaction for those who work in long-term care. She is an avid advocate and consultant for the industry challenges that face today's health care agencies. Dr. Stewart's recent publications and research include *The Investigation of the Preferred Learning Styles of Persons Living with Dementia, Caregivers' Attitudes and Beliefs about Pain Medication Administration, Finding the Good in the Workplace Bully,* and *Bullies do not Work Alone.*

INDEX

A

Adams's equity theory, 71
assessments, organizational, 12-13
attention deficit disorder (ADD), 68-69
attention deficit hyperactivity disorder (ADHD), 68-69

B

behaviors, victim, 48-49, 52
bully, 2-7, 9, 15-16, 18, 33-37, 39-41, 44-48, 55-55, 58, 60, 63, 71,
    94-96
    workplace, 1-2, 9, 11, 24, 14, 63
bully behavior, 39-41, 55
bully events, 2,9, 16, 20, 95-96
bullying, 3-5, 10, 15-22, 24, 27, 33, 36, 41, 43, 45-46, 54-58, 64-65, 69,
    83-84, 86, 88-90, 92
    organizational definition of, 20
    workplace, 7-10, 20, 51, 55, 59
bully triads, 7, 9-11, 15, 18-20, 22-26, 35, 47-50, 54, 56-57, 62-64, 70,
    74-75, 76, 96-97,
burnout, 3, 12,17, 46, 50, 52, 60, 63, 66, 80
bystander effect, 58
bystanders, 3, 5, 7, 15-16, 54-59, 97

I

innovation, 5, 31, 39-40, 44, 46, 50, 52, 68-70, 73

M

mental health, 19, 42, 66, 88
mental health issues, 41-42
motivation, job, 71

N

needs assessment, 11, 13, 22
new insights communication inventory (NICI), 37

O

O'Grady, Dennis, 6, 8, 10, 37, 43, 47, 51
organizational culture assessment instrument (OCAI), 12

P

performance, organizational, 12
personalities, bully-type, 2
policies, 7, 12, 16-17, 20, 29, 38-40, 44, 49, 52, 57, 60, 62, 69-71, 79-80, 83, 97
posttraumatic stress disorder (PTSD), 46, 50, 52
productivity, 1, 4, 19, 33, 45, 54, 68-69, 78, 82, 97, 99
    low, 83
programs
    recognition, 19-20, 36, 41, 44, 52, 65, 68, 70-71
    reward, 19-20, 36, 44, 52, 65, 68, 70-71
psychometric testing, 42, 44, 50, 53

R

recognition, 19-20, 33, 36, 41, 44, 48, 50, 52, 57, 63, 65, 68-71
return on investment (ROI), 62, 65
rewards, 19, 29-30, 35-36, 38, 41, 47-50, 57, 65, 70-71
rubrics, 26, 28

S

self-efficacy scale (GSE), 4, 8, 44, 48, 52, 60
silo thinking, 18, 35, 61
socialization, 37-38, 74
structure, organizational, 2, 4, 12, 40, 68
Studer Group, 66
survey, needs assessment, 11

T

testing
    EQ, 70
    IQ, 70

V

victims, 3-5, 7, 15-16, 18, 38-39, 45-48, 54, 97
    behaviors of, 35

W

wellness, organizational, 6-7, 15, 74-75
whistle-blowing, 56
Witte, Bill, 74
workplace environment, 1, 3, 7, 20, 54, 29, 61
workplaces, toxic, 10,15
workplace wellness initiatives, 26

www.ingramcontent.com/pod-product-compliance
Lightning Source LLC
Chambersburg PA
CBHW022102020426
42335CB00012B/793